SCREAM

SCREAM

THE UNOFFICIAL GUIDE TO THE SCREAM TRILOGY

JOHN BROSNAN

BOXTREE

First published 2000 by Boxtree
an imprint of Macmillan Publishers Ltd
25 Eccleston Place London SW1W 9NF
Basingstoke and Oxford

www.macmillan.co.uk

Associated companies throughout the world

ISBN 0 7522 7162 8

1 3 5 7 9 8 6 4 2

A CIP catalogue record for this book is available from the British Library.

Designed by Blackjacks
Printed by Mackays of Chatham plc

Picture Acknowledgements: 1, Steve Granitz/Retna Pictures; 2 (top) Tim
Hale/Retna Pictures; 2, (bottom left) Bill Davila/Retna Pictures; 2 (bottom right)
Dave Lewis/Rex Features; 3 (top) Armando Gallo/Retna Pictures; 3 (bottom left)
Kimberly Butler/London Features International; 3 (bottom right) Steve
Granitz/Retna Pictures; 4 (top) John Spellman/Retna Pictures; 4 (bottom) Erik
Pendzich/Rex Features; 5 (top left) Bruce Birmelin/Rex Features; 5 (top right)
Retna Pictures; 5 (bottom) Allen Gordon/London Features International; 6 (top)
David Fisher/London Features International; 6 (bottom) Phil Loftus/Capital
Pictures; 7 (top) Pat Pope/Rex Features; 7 (bottom) Anita Weber/Capital
Pictures; 8 (top) Bruce Birmelin/Rex Features; 8 (bottom) Retna.

CONTENTS

With special thanks to Bill Warren

SCREAM

'You like scary movies?'

SCREAM
THE MOVIE

The film opens with a close-up of a ringing cellphone. It's answered by a teenage girl, Casey Becker, fresh-faced and cheerful, with a blonde page-boy haircut and wearing a white woolly sweater. She hears a man's voice on the phone asking who she is. She tells him he's got a wrong number and hangs up. She's amused. The phone rings again. It's the same caller. This time he says he wants to talk. With a smile, she tells him there are 0900 numbers for that and hangs up again. The camera then reveals that Casey's house is an isolated one in the country and surrounded by trees. There's a swing hanging from the branch of one of the trees. The camera also reveals that the ground floor of the brightly-lit house has a lot of large windows...

Casey is preparing popcorn on the stove when the phone rings again. Same caller. He asks why she doesn't want to talk to him. Still amused, she asks him his name. He says he'll tell her his name if she tells him hers. She declines. Then the caller hears the cooking popcorn and asks what the noise is. Casey tells him, adding that she's getting ready to watch a video. When he asks what video, she replies that it's just some scary movie. 'You like scary movies?' asks the caller.

Casey, still amused by this chance phone encounter, tells him that she does. She is moving from room to room now, carrying the cellphone with her. When he asks her what her favourite horror movie is, she says it's *Halloween*. Then she asks him his favourite and he tells her to guess. She says *A Nightmare on Elm Street*. The caller says he liked that movie. It was scary. She says that the first one was, but that the rest 'sucked'. Then he asks her if she has a boyfriend. Casey is almost flirting with him now and asks him if he wants to ask her out on a date. He asks her again if she has a boyfriend and she says she hasn't. When he asks her what her name is again and she asks him why he wants to know, he replies that he wants to know who he's looking at.

At this point Casey becomes alarmed. She switches on the outside patio lights and stares through the glass patio doors. Beyond we see the swimming pool and the trees. There's no sign of anyone. She locks the patio doors and asks the caller what he wants. He says he just wants to talk. She cuts him off. He rings back, saying he thought they were going to go out together. Frightened now, she tells him to call someone else and hangs up. He calls back, sounding very angry, and warns her that if she hangs up on him again he'll gut her like a fish. She asks him if this is some sort of a joke. 'More like a game' is his reply. She hangs up again. Then the front doorbell rings. She calls out, 'Who's there?!' And the caller rings back, telling her she should never say that in a situation like this. If she watched scary movies she should know that. Does she have a death wish? Casey then threatens him with her boyfriend, saying that he'll be arriving at any moment. The caller is unimpressed and asks her if her boyfriend's name is Steve. She wants to know how he knows that. The caller tells her to turn on the patio lights again. Casey does, looks out and is shocked to see Steve, his face bloody, tied to a chair with his mouth taped shut.

The caller then tells Casey he wants to play a game. And if she refuses to play then Steve will die immediately. It's a movie trivia quiz. If she gets the right answer, Steve lives. But first he gives her a warm-up question: Who is the killer in *Halloween*? She gets it right – Michael Myers. Then it's time for the real question. Name the killer in *Friday the 13th*. Now nearly hysterical, Casey says it was Jason. Wrong answer, the killer informs her. 'It was Jason!' screams Casey. 'I saw that movie twenty goddamn times!' Then you should know, the killer tells her, that it was Mrs Voorhees, Jason's mother. 'Jason didn't turn up until the sequel.' Fearfully, Casey turns on the patio lights again. She sees that Steve is now dead. He's been gutted.

The caller has a final question for her: 'What door am I at?'

Then a chair comes crashing in through a window. Terrified, Casey flees into the kitchen and spots a black-robed figure moving across the sitting-room. She grabs a kitchen knife and then slips out through the patio doors. Outside she sees the lights of her parents' approaching car. She turns back to the window – and finds herself staring right into the killer's masked face. He smashes the window, tries to grab her, and she hits him with the cellphone. She starts to run but the killer catches up with her and stabs her in the chest. Her parents' car pulls up in the driveway and they get out. Casey hits the killer with the phone again and crawls through the garden towards them. She tries to call out, but the blade has punctured her lung and she can only make wheezing sounds. Oblivious, her parents go into the house.

The killer attacks Casey again. Dying, she reaches for his mask and pulls it off – but only Casey sees the face behind the mask. And then she is stabbed again.

Inside the house her parents realize something is wrong. They try calling the police but over the phone they can only hear the sounds made by the dying Casey as she is dragged across the lawn by the killer. Her father tells his wife to drive to their nearest neighbour and get help. But when the mother steps outside she screams in horror.

Hanging from the ropes of the tree-swing is Casey's gutted – and very dead – body. Then the titles and credits of the movie start to roll, heralding not only the beginning of *Scream* but a whole new chapter in the horror film genre…

Every few years the horror film is pronounced dead, then along comes a movie that revives the corpse and once again the genre is alive and kicking. *Scream* was such a movie. In 1996 it not only revived the genre but completely re-invented horror movies. And it was that rare thing, a horror film with a sense of humour without being an outright spoof. It was also the first true post-modernist horror movie – a movie that deconstructed itself as it went along.

Scream was the work of veteran horror director Wes Craven and a new young writer, Kevin Williamson. It turned out to be a happy combination of their talents, Craven in particular producing a work that was far superior to his recent directorial efforts. As well as being a polished and clever movie, *Scream* also had the advantage of inspired casting, most notably in the case of the two leading female characters, played by Neve Campbell and Courteney Cox. Both had appeared in feature films before, but it was their respective hit TV shows, *Party of Five* and *Friends* – and the large fan base they had each amassed as a result – which became an important factor in the film's success. Campbell and Cox were backed by a talented group of young actors, many of them relatively unknown at the time despite their experience, such as David Arquette, Jamie Kennedy, Matthew Lillard, Rose McGowan and Skeet Ulrich, along with more established players like Drew Barrymore and Henry Winkler (the 'Fonz' from TV's *Happy Days*). *Scream* became the surprise box-office hit of 1996–7, clicking not only with the horror fans but also with a much wider audience. After opening slowly at first in America when it was released in December 1996, it went on to make over $100 million by June 1997. For a horror movie to make that kind of money was extremely unusual.

Scream was a breakthrough horror movie on many levels but its most obvious innovation was in the way it treated the conventions of the genre. A familiar criticism of traditional horror films is the way the characters in the film behave. No one in previous horror films ever seems to have seen a horror film before, with the result that they do really *stupid* things. We've all had the experience of watching a horror movie on TV where you start yelling advice at the screen along the lines of: 'No, don't go in there *alone*, you idiot! My God, I don't believe anyone can be that idiotic! Oops... serves you right...' What *Scream* did was to take this failing and turn it on its head. Not only are many of the characters in *Scream* cinema-literate but some of them seem to *know* they're in a horror film. And that generates a large part of the film's fun: it plays on our expectations and continually subverts them. In a sense, *Scream* is set within a self-contained world that appears to follow the established rules of a horror film. Certain characters are familiar with these rules and this seems to provide them with a survival advantage, but the problem is that the killers know the rules better than anyone else does... and they're cheating.

Significantly, it's the heroine, Sidney (Neve Campbell), who is unwilling to accept the importance of horror movies. When she gets a call from the killer, whom she mistakes for her boyfriend, Billy (who in the end does turn out to be one of the killers), and he asks the inevitable question about liking scary movies, she replies that they're all the same. 'Some stupid killer stalking some big-breasted girl who can't act and who keeps running up the stairs when she should be going out the front door.' And very soon after this unwise denial of the relevance of horror movies she finds herself in precisely the same situation as one of those girls...

Later, in a bedroom sequence with her boyfriend, Billy Loomis (Skeet Ulrich), shortly before she allows herself to be seduced by him she tells him she's afraid she's going to turn out to be a 'bad seed' like her murdered mother. Billy responds by saying she's like Jodie Foster in *Silence of the Lambs* when she's having flashbacks of her dead father. Sidney insists that it's real life, not a movie. But Billy replies, 'Sure it is, Sid... It's all one great big movie.' He adds that you get to pick your genre. Sidney sighs that she'd prefer to be in a Meg Ryan movie.

That Billy defines himself and his world entirely in cinematic terms is emphasized in another, earlier bedroom sequence. Billy, having sneaked into Sidney's room, compares their relationship to a television version of *The Exorcist*; i.e. that it's been edited for its sexual content. (This is not *Scream*'s only reference to *The Exorcist*; Linda Blair, the star of that film, has a brief cameo as a reporter.)

The character who seems to know all the answers, because he apparently knows more about horror films than anyone else, is Randy (Jamie Kennedy). Randy works part-time in a video store (it's mentioned that he got the sack from the local Blockbusters) and is the ultimate movie geek. However, any similarity between him and Quentin Tarantino would surely be coincidental – if it wasn't for the fact that Tarantino's films were clearly one of the many inspirations for *Scream*. In a sequence in the video shop, when Randy is discussing the first murder and the subsequent attack on Sidney with his friend Stuart (Matthew Lillard), he says that Billy is clearly the murderer because he's got 'killer' written all over him. Stuart asks him why the cops let Billy go and Randy replies that it's because they don't watch enough horror movies. Stuart isn't convinced and asks why Billy would want to kill his own girlfriend. Randy replies that there's always 'some stupid bullshit reason' for someone to kill their girlfriend. He adds, 'Besides, if it's too complicated, you lose your target audience.'

It's Randy who delivers the keynote lecture about horror films during the big party sequence in which he establishes the rules you have to follow if you want to live through a horror movie. 'Rule number one – you can never have sex… sex equals death. Number two – you can never drink or do drugs. It's the sin factor – it's an extension of number one. And number three – never, ever, *ever* under any circumstances say, "I'll be right back." Because you won't be back. You push the laws and you end up dead.' However, this warning comes too late for Sidney's best friend, Tatum (Rose McGowan), who has already made a fatal journey downstairs to fetch more drinks from the garage. There she has encountered Ghostface. Thinking it's Randy playing a joke on her, she says to him, 'What movie is this from? *I Spit on Your Garage?*' Then, still thinking it's a game, she begs 'Mr Ghostface' not to kill her because she wants to be in the sequel. Alas, she meets a very nasty, if ingenious, end. While trying to escape through the doggy-flap in the garage door, she gets stuck. And when the killer activates the door's electric motor and it begins to slide upwards, the struggling Tatum goes with it. The result is a broken neck when she is jammed between the door and the garage ceiling. In a way this scene is even more shocking than the gory attack on Casey at the start of the film.

'That garage scene certainly works,' said Craven. 'Our preview audiences really felt a sense of shock, like they couldn't believe that

Tatum dies. They'd come to like the character so much, and after her death a sort of strange hush fell over the audience. Staging-wise, it's a very interesting scene. There's a lot of suspense, a jump, then a protracted struggle, and finally the death, so it's a sort of set-piece.'

The horror films on which the rules in *Scream* are based belong to a particular category within the horror genre: the splatter/slash movies such as the *Friday the 13th* series, *Prom Night*, *Terror Train*, *A Stranger Calls* (the prologue involving Casey and the mystery phone caller is clearly a homage to the latter film), and even Craven's own *A Nightmare on Elm Street* (there's a neat in-joke when the school principal, played by Henry Winkler, briefly encounters the school janitor 'Fred', who is dressed similarly to Freddy Kruger and was played by Craven himself). But the most important cinematic template is *Halloween*, the 1978 John Carpenter classic that started the whole trend. *Halloween* provided writer Kevin Williamson with the central inspiration for *Scream*. 'I would play the soundtracks from all the *Halloween*s while I was writing the script,' he said. 'Because *Halloween* was a catalyst for it all. My movie is a kind of homage to it.' Oddly enough, Craven himself isn't much of a fan of *Halloween*, though he admires it on a technical level.

A sequence from *Halloween* plays a key role in *Scream* when the high school students are watching the film on TV at a party – the prelude to the final, and extended, bout of bloody slaughter. As ever, Randy, the movie geek, is showing off his knowledge of movie trivia. As a victim is stabbed in *Halloween*, Stuart announces that he wants to see Jamie Lee Curtis's breasts, and Randy says, 'Not until *Trading Places* in 1983. Jamie Lee was always a virgin in horror movies. She never showed her tits until she went legits. That's why she always outsmarted the killer in the big chase scene at the end. Only virgins can do that.'

Amusingly, this is intercut with Sidney – still a virgin at this point – and Billy preparing to make love upstairs in a bedroom. And when Randy points to the TV screen and announces that the obligatory tit shot is about to appear, there's a cut to Sidney taking off her shirt, but she's wearing a bra. (When she takes the bra off, the shot is blocked by Billy's body, sending a clear message to the viewer: like

Jamie Lee Curtis before her, Neve Campbell has high standards when it comes to refusing to do nude scenes in horror movies.)

The party sequence and its aftermath are very cleverly handled – a real cinematic *tour de force*. In terms of playing with the concept of a film within a film, within *another* film, it goes about as far as you can possibly go, for while the students are watching *Halloween* they are themselves being filmed. Earlier the TV reporter Gale Weathers (Courteney Cox) had surreptitiously placed a mini TV camera on top of the TV set. As a result, the students are being watched by Gale and her cameraman Kenny (W. Earl Brown) on a TV monitor in their outside-broadcast van parked in front of the house. And, of course, in the larger context they are actors being filmed. As an ingenious addition to the sense of dislocation, there's a thirty-second delay between the events taking place in the sitting-room and the images appearing on the van's TV monitor. Later, when the others have gone and Randy is left on his own to watch *Halloween*, Kenny, now joined by Sid who is on the run from the killer (Gale having gone off with Deputy Dwight, telling Kenny 'I'll be right back' as she left), sees the masked murderer appear behind the oblivious Randy. Randy is yelling at the TV, 'Jamie, look behind you!' as the killer brandishes a knife behind *him*. Kenny forgets about the thirty-second delay, starts to leave the van to warn Randy... and walks straight into the killer, who promptly cuts his throat (a moment which cries out for the line, 'Ohmigod, they've killed Kenny!').

But *Scream* is more than just a collection of clever movie in-jokes; it also works as an effective horror movie in its own right. The attacks by the hooded killer are well staged and genuinely unsettling, and their impact is aided by the distinctive mask the killer wears. (The choice of the mask – the 'Ghostface' – was an almost last-minute decision by the film-makers. Legend has it that Craven had a fortuitous encounter with someone wearing one at a Halloween party, of all things, but this, alas, is just a legend – see 'Behind the Scenes of *Scream*' for the full story). Most importantly, *Scream* keeps you guessing almost until the end about the identity of the killer. The nature of the killer, incidentally, is where *Scream* seriously parts company with

Halloween. In that film Michael Myers, a.k.a. 'the Shape', is provided with supernatural properties that become more obvious as the story progresses; by the end of the film he has been transformed into the true 'bogeyman' of childhood nightmares, an unkillable entity who finally vanishes into thin air. *Scream* teases you with the possibility that 'Ghostface' is a supernatural creature, mainly because he seems to possess the uncanny ability to be in two places at the same time, but in the end it is revealed that there are actually *two* killers: a double-act consisting of Billy Loomis (Loomis was the name of Donald Pleasance's character in *Halloween*, incidentally) and Stuart.

And then there's the question of motive. Earlier, in the sequence in the video store where Randy, Billy and Stuart are speculating about the killer, Stuart says, understandably in the light of what we later learn about him, that he thinks it's Sidney's father Neil (Lawrence Hecht), who's gone suspiciously missing. He asks Randy why the police can't find Mr Prescott. Randy replies that he's probably dead already and that his body will turn up in the last reel, horribly mutilated. He explains that it can all be boiled down to a simple formula, which is: 'Everybody's a suspect!' Billy then accuses Randy of being a likely suspect himself. Randy agrees: 'If this was a scary movie I'd be the prime suspect.' And when Stuart asks him what his motive would be, Randy says, 'Motives are incidental.' This point about an apparent lack of motive behind the murderers' actions is repeated in the film's penultimate climactic sequence when, after Billy and Stuart have revealed themselves to Sidney, she asks why they murdered her mother (and everyone else) and Billy says that they don't really believe in motives, adding that no one ever found out why Hannibal Lecter likes to eat people. 'See, it's a lot scarier when there's no motive, Sid.'

This seeming lack of motives leads to an interesting subtext in *Scream*, that of the possible gay element running below the surface of the story. When Williamson came out early in 1999, and in the light of the homoeroticism perceived in his TV series, *Dawson's Creek* and *Wasteland*, some critics took another look at *Scream* in order to see if it contained any overtly gay reference points. And indeed it may do. The concept of two young men committing murder for the sheer thrill of it relates directly to the famous Leopold–Loeb murder case of the 1920s. Leopold and Loeb, who were lovers, murdered a third young man, a friend of theirs, as a kind of intellectual, Nietzschean exercise. The case became the basis for Alfred Hitchcock's *Rope* (1948), which featured Farley Granger and John Dall as the two murderers (the gay element, though present, was greatly downplayed), as well as two other films, *Compulsion* and *Swoon*. Reinforcing this theory is the fact that though Billy and Stuart in *Scream* are ostensibly heterosexual, they appear to have no emotional attachment at all to their respective girlfriends. Of course, Billy was out to kill Sidney all along as part of his grand plan but, while we don't know which of them killed Tatum in the garage, it's suggested that it could have easily been her boyfriend Stuart under the mask. Plus there is the sequence at the climax where the two young men take turns to stab each other with the knife in an act of almost ritualistic sado-masochistic mutilation. But it's only in *Scream 2*, when Randy, taunting the killer on his cellphone, describes Billy Loomis as a 'homo-repressed mother's boy', that there is any overt mention of this subtext. In any event, this speculation remains another interesting strand in the on-going game of deconstructing *Scream*, a film which is in itself an act of deconstruction.

But when it comes to the final question of motives, Williamson has it both ways. Despite the duo's claim that they are committing a truly motiveless crime, Williamson also provides Billy with an actual motive: it turns out he hated Sidney's mother because she had an affair with his father. It broke up his parents' marriage and his mother abandoned him as a result. 'Parental abandonment causes serious deviant behaviour,' he tells Sidney. 'Certainly fucked you up. It made you have sex with a psychopath.' And Stuart points out that as she's no longer a virgin, she's forfeited her horror movie right to protection. She has to die now because those are the rules.

The witty movie references continue right through the climax of *Scream*. After Stuart and Billy have carried out their mutual stabbing in order to seem like victims of the killer, Stuart, bleeding profusely, tells Sidney that everyone is going to die except him and Billy because they have to stay around to plan the sequel. Sidney calls them sick and says they've seen too many movies, but Billy says they're not to blame. 'Movies don't create psychos! Movies make psychos more creative!' And then he stabs Stuart again.

Later, when Sidney has gained the upper hand and called the police, the question of motives is raised again. She asks Stuart over the phone what his motive is, seeing that Billy has one. Amusingly, he tells her that it's all down to peer pressure. Then, still dripping copious amounts of blood due to Billy's over-enthusiastic work with the knife, he asks Sidney if she really called the police. When Sidney confirms that she has, he sobs, 'Oh...my mom and dad are going to be so mad at me.'

Despite his wounds he manages a final, spirited attack on Sidney, pinning her to the floor and telling her he's always fancied her (a last-minute declaration of heterosexuality, perhaps?). She dispatches him appropriately, by dropping the TV set on his head just as it's showing the climax of *Halloween*. 'In your dreams,' she says, as he spectacularly expires with an explosion of sparks.

Randy, having been shot by Billy and presumed dead by both Sidney and the audience, makes a surprise reappearance at the end (one of many) and declares himself happy to be a virgin. Still a stickler for the rules of the horror genre, Randy points out that though Billy seems to be dead (after being shot by Gale Weathers who has also made a last-minute surprise reappearance) this is the time when the supposedly dead killer comes back to life. And on cue Billy suddenly sits up... only to be shot in the head by Sidney, who says firmly, 'Not in my movie.'

SCREAM
BEHIND THE SCENES

Scream began life as a screenplay called *Scary Movie*, the work of Kevin Williamson, who'd been a struggling actor in New York before deciding to move to LA and try his luck in Hollywood as a screenwriter. Already there are differing versions of the actual circumstances under which he wrote it: one has it that he borrowed a friend's house in Palm Springs and produced the screenplay over one 'sleepless' weekend, while the other version has him locking himself in a Palm Springs hotel room and writing *Scary Movie* over a three-day period. At least it's safe to assume that Palm Springs figured somewhere in the story.

According to Williamson, he got the original idea from watching a TV special about a real-life murder case. 'I was house-sitting for a friend to pay him back for money he'd lent me for groceries and I thought I heard something. It scared the hell out of me. I was wandering around the house with a knife and a cellphone, and I called another friend. We got into a long discussion about horror movies and started testing each other on them. And that's how *Scream* was born.'

Actually, at this stage *Scary Movie* consisted of just one long 25-page sequence about someone alone in a house being menaced by a threatening presence. Williamson told *Cinefantastique* magazine: 'I thought if I could just add a story onto this terrifying 25-page sequence, I could probably sell it to Roger Corman for $5,000. I had friends who were making Roger Corman films, and I'd even acted in a couple of them, so that was my initial game plan.'

After he'd written the screenplay Williamson decided it had so many horror in-jokes that only horror movie enthusiasts would appreciate it. He was even reluctant to send it to his agents. 'I was too scared to give it to the head agent, so I gave it to the junior agent instead.' While he waited for a reaction he wrote a synopsis for a sequel, and even started writing the opening sequence of the second screenplay. After an anxious few days of waiting, his agents responded positively and told him they could do a lot better than Roger Corman. Very soon an auction was under way among several leading Hollywood companies, including Universal, Paramount, Miramax, Morgan Creek and Oliver Stone's production company. For Williamson it was every budding scriptwriter's fantasy come to life.

Though Miramax didn't initially make the biggest offer, Williamson instinctively thought he would be better off becoming involved with them, especially as he felt he had a rapport with Miramax boss, Bob Weinstein. 'Oliver Stone's company offered more money,' said Williamson, 'but there was no guarantee that Stone would make it right away. It might have sat on the backburner for years or it might not have got made at all.' After his disappointing experience with his first screenplay, *Killing Mrs Tingle* (he was removed from his own project and replaced by other writers), he finally opted for the company that was showing the greatest enthusiasm for the project – Miramax, whose subdivision, Dimension Films, was devoted to genre movies.

'Bob Weinstein and the small group of people that surround him all have a love of genre films; they all have a love for the movies that I love.' Miramax paid Williamson $500,000 plus box-office points for *Scary Movie* (the title was changed to *Scream* when some obscure Texas film-maker objected to their use of the original title). And, almost as important for him, they were as good as their word about their commitment to the project: exactly one year after they'd bought it, the movie had been completed.

Bob Weinstein and Miramax were also instrumental in securing the involvement of another player who turned out to be a vital contributor to the success story that *Scream* became – the director Wes Craven. The creator of the innovative *A Nightmare on Elm Street*, Craven had been working with Miramax on a planned remake of the 1963 *The Haunting*, but when none of the drafts of the new screenplay proved acceptable to Weinstein and his colleagues, the company let their option drop. (It was immediately picked up by Dreamworks and eventually turned into a lamentable movie by *Speed* director Jan De Bont.) Anxious to stay involved with Craven, Miramax offered *Scream* to him… and he turned it down. One reason was that he was not too impressed with Williamson's first draft of the screenplay; the other reason was that he wanted to disengage himself from the horror movie genre. 'I thought this was not a film I wanted to do because I'd been trying to get away from making shocking horror films.' But then, after the script had been rewritten, he took another look at it and changed his mind. 'Finally, I just thought it was really worth it. It was sort of like being shown the script to *Pulp Fiction*. You just don't read scripts like this very often. It's wickedly funny and scary and a lot of things all at once.'

Williamson was pleased when Craven finally came on board. After Craven had turned it down, various other directors were considered, including Robert Rodriguez (who would later direct Williamson's *The Faculty*), Danny Boyle and George Junng. Then Bob Weinstein called Williamson to tell him that Craven was going to direct his screenplay. 'I was really thrilled', said Williamson, 'because I really loved *A Nightmare on Elm Street*.'

It's also likely that Craven had become aware of the excited buzz that the script was generating around Hollywood by that time. Already Miramax had signed up Drew Barrymore for a small but important role, and then Courteney Cox, fresh from the success of TV's *Friends*, declared herself willing to join the *Scream* team (at one point Sharon Stone had let it be known that she was interested in the role of Gale Weathers). Craven would have been guilty of a serious lapse of judgement if he hadn't taken notice of these signs that *Scream* promised to be something out of the ordinary. Besides, his career needed a boost, even if it did mean making another horror film. He'd recently had a bad experience with the Eddie Murphy vehicle, *Vampire in Brooklyn* which had done neither his nor Murphy's career any favours.

The casting of *Scream* was another important factor in its subsequent success. From his own experience Craven knew that doing a film featuring mainly teenagers limits you to actors of a certain age group, which often means a lack of acting experience. This was not the case with *Scream*. 'I was really struck by the way Miramax went for relatively well-known and highly paid actors,' said Craven. 'Usually a studio will say, "Here's your casting budget, get whoever you can." But Courteney Cox wasn't cheap, and some of the kids brought considerable fees to the budget.' Neve Campbell, who played the heroine Sidney, had come from TV's popular up-market soap, *Party of Five* and had had one previous big film role in *The Craft* (1996), a supernatural thriller about four young witches. David Arquette (Deputy Dewey), brother of Rosanna, Patricia, Richmond and Alexis, had recently appeared in another Miramax production, the comedy-drama *Beautiful Girls* (1996) and back in 1992 had had a small role in the original *Buffy the Vampire Slayer* movie. Skeet Ulrich (Sidney's boyfriend Billy – and one of the killers) had had a leading role in Paul Schrader's *The Touch* and also appeared with Neve Campbell in *The Craft*. 'There were a lot of actors who would have been much cheaper than Skeet', said Craven, 'but nobody could nail the role like he did. When he came in, suddenly six weeks of casting went out the window, because he really understood the part. It was a lot more money, but well worth it.' Matthew Lillard (who played Stuart, the other killer) had been in *Hackers* (1995). Rose McGowan (Tatum) had appeared in the cult success *The Doom Generation* (1995). Jamie Kennedy (Randy) was the only virtual newcomer, his previous experience being mainly in stand-up comedy. Together they made an above-average acting ensemble.

Once the production got under way, Craven was quick to appreciate the quality of his cast. 'There's a great deal of talent here,' he told *Fangoria* magazine on the set of *Scream*. 'Many of them are quite new to me. I didn't know Rose or David's work until about a month before casting. They're very bright kids; they have incredible inventiveness.' And at the end of the shoot he was still singing their praises:

They're very skilled actors who brought an immense amount to the set. Matthew Lillard got into it with incredible ferocity and Skeet Ulrich really nailed his character. I told Neve at the beginning, 'This is going to be an incredibly physical role and very emotional. You'd better prepare for that.' And she just gave one thousand percent every day. There was a tremendous amount of running, fight scenes, falling, climbing over rooftops and a constant high emotional pitch all the time for some fifty days but Neve and the others all threw themselves into it with incredible enthusiasm. There was a lot of invention from the actors, who were very much into the film and having a good time.

When asked if all the members of the large cast had behaved themselves, he diplomatically replied, 'Nobody was a pain in the ass. There's always the potential for star tantrums, somebody being a real bitch on wheels, but it didn't happen. It was a love-fest. We all had a hoot. We were very organized but at the same time we ran a very relaxed and loving and supportive set.'

Admittedly there was some confusion among a few of the cast members during the shoot as to exactly what kind of movie they were making. For example, David Arquette, when interviewed on the set by *Fangoria* magazine, said that the film was 'real spoofy' and that he played Deputy Dewey for laughs. 'Wes allowed me to go with my comedy angle on the character. I'm a little cartoony. I was in *Buffy the Vampire Slayer*, which was supposed to be spoofy, but *Scream* is the movie that *Buffy* wishes it was.' However, Craven had a somewhat different take on Arquette's character, not to mention the movie itself: 'There's a deputy in the film who is very clever and smart… at the beginning he looks like the stupid deputy but he really is a human being. *Scream* is not a spoof. It operates on a more sophisticated level than satire. I don't know where the idea that it's a spoof came from.'

Cinefantastique writer Lawrence French was visiting the *Scream* set on the day that *The Exorcist* star Linda Blair was doing her brief cameo, as a pushy reporter, with Neve Campbell and David Arquette, and his description of the scene provides an insight into Arquette's somewhat off-beat approach to his role. The scene called for Arquette, as Deputy 'Dewey' Riley, to escort Campbell into the school while shielding her from Blair's unwanted attention. Arquette's line to Blair was supposed to be, 'Leave the kid alone. She just wants to go to school.' Said Lawrence, 'On the second take Arquette has flubbed his line, and on subsequent shots he seems to be doing improvised variations of the line. Craven watched calmly... before taking Arquette gently aside and conferring with him privately.' Lawrence later asked the director if he'd been annoyed by the delay. Craven denied it:

David is so loveable, I couldn't get mad at him. There have been a couple of times where I had to say, 'Let's get professional here,' but David, more than anyone else, marches to a different drummer, and that comes across in his performance. You get something very special and unique. Part of it is because he doesn't memorize his lines completely. He told me, 'I start losing something if I know all the lines.'... As the director, I could threaten him and say, 'You must know the lines exactly as they're written,' but you can get into a whole power struggle that way. I don't feel compelled to do that, because he's giving us something delightful.

Perhaps Arquette was distracted by his blossoming romance with his co-star, Courteney Cox, as the relationship that led to their marriage in 1999 began during the shooting of the first *Scream*.

Scream was shot on a budget of $14 million over a two-month period at locations in Sonoma County in northern California. Originally, Williamson had set the story in North Carolina, where he grew up, but though Craven initially scouted for locations in that area, he didn't feel the architecture was suitable. He wanted the houses in the film to look as 'American' as possible, and eventually found exactly what he wanted in northern California. Parts of three different towns, Santa Rosa, Healdsburg and Tomales, were used to create the fictional town of Woodsboro. The house at the beginning of the film, where Casey (Drew Barrymore) is terrorized and then butchered by the killer, was a private residence in the wine country of Glen Ellen. And for the film's lengthy – and bloody – climax, which took 22 days to shoot, Craven used an abandoned house on a 200-acre ranch near the town of Tomales, some 45 minutes to the north-west of San Francisco, and only a few miles from Bodega Bay, where Alfred Hitchcock shot *The Birds*. 'The house we found was actually brand new,' said Craven. 'It had not been quite completed when both of the owners died. The young family who inherited didn't quite know what to do with it. They were very happy to let us use it.' The film's designer, Bruce Miller, was particularly happy with it because of its large size. He said, 'It just doesn't make sense that, in a normal American home, murders could be happening in the upstairs bedrooms and the people watching TV downstairs wouldn't know about it.'

Healdsburg police station stood in for the Woodsboro police station and, for the fictional Woodsboro High School, the film-makers planned to use the real-life Santa Rosa High School, for a long time a popular setting with other film-makers because it personifies the ideal concept of an American high school. However, after reading the *Scream* screenplay, members of the school board raised objections, and permission for the unit to use the school was withdrawn at the last moment. One of their main objections was a line of dialogue spoken by the school principal (Henry Winkler) when he is berating a couple of students who have been caught running around the corridors dressed in the same costume as the killer: 'a fair punishment would be to rip your insides out and hang you from a tree so you can be exposed for the desensitized, heartless little shits that you are!' The board also disapproved of *Scream*'s content: they didn't want their school to be associated with a film about two high-schoolboy students who go about murdering their fellow students, not to mention several other people. (In the light of the subsequent massacre at the Columbine High School in Denver, the board no doubt feel that their decision in 1996 has been vindicated – see 'The Gore, the Censors and the Backlash' pages 32–6 for more on this subject.)

Craven was not happy with their decision or the reasons for which it was taken.

They were being hypocritical reactionaries. It was really scary, like when they were hanging witches in Salem, because there was that same sort of hysteria. But the most disappointing thing about the incident was the side of the American psyche it revealed. There was some petty and nasty caricaturing of horror films. The local newspaper never referred to Scream as just a film but always as some gory horror film with foul language. The school board kept talking about the foul-mouthed principal, but all he says is 'you little shits'. That was it, certainly nothing your typical school student hasn't heard before.

The attacks in the local paper also got personal as far as Craven was concerned.

They said things like, 'Wes Craven and his money-grabbing friends from Hollywood have come here to buy our morals and corrupt our children.' It was scary, because not only was I singled out and attacked personally, but there was such a conspiratorial feeling of, 'You're not going to be allowed to practice your craft here. You're too evil, and we're going to stop you. It doesn't matter whether it's legal or not, because it's a moral issue.' Once it becomes an issue of morality, then all logic goes out the window and you feel like, 'two more steps to the right, and people will be knocking on your door in the middle of the night...' It was chilling.

Nor was it easy to find a substitute setting for the school. The newspaper attacks had been circulated in neighbouring communities and no sooner did the film company show an interest in shooting in any of them than local opposition would immediately spring up.

'Church ministers and different organizations would get petitions up against us,' said Craven. 'And 90% of the attacks we had were by people who hadn't read the script. It really was like a nightmare!' The film-makers were finally obliged to use the Sonoma Community Center, which had been a school but was now owned by a private group that rented it out to community organizations. The building therefore wasn't under the same kind of jurisdictions as a public one. There was still some local opposition to the idea but the filming went ahead. It was estimated that the loss of the Santa Rosa school and the lengthy search for an alternative setting cost Miramax in the region of $350,000.

Another key task in the filming of *Scream* was to establish the right look for the killer(s). In the original screenplay the killer was simply described as wearing a ghost-mask, but finding a suitable mask proved difficult. It was simply by luck that producer Marianne Maddalena spotted a mask in a child's bedroom at a house they were checking out as a possible location. She showed it to Craven, who immediately said, 'That's it!' The mask was turned over to the KNB EFX Group, who were handling the make-up effects, in the hope that they could alter the design to the extent that it would become copyright free. However, their suggested variations to the original mask just didn't have the same impact. 'It was uncanny,' said Craven, 'but the unknown artist who sculpted this mask had just caught something. Luckily we found the manufacturer's name printed inside the mask. We managed to get the rights to use it literally the day after we started shooting.'

The manufacturers were a company called Fun World and the 'unknown artist' was Fun World employee Brigitte Sleiertin. 'The idea is something I worked on with Allan Geller, the vice-president of the company,' Sleiertin told *Fangoria* magazine. 'We came up with an assortment of masks that had a ghostface look and that particular design was the strangest one.' According to Geller, 'What attracted Craven to it was that it was a multifaceted look. It's not just horror… it's a horrible look, a sorry look, a frantic look.' And, of course, it bears a striking resemblance to Edvard Munch's famous painting, *The Scream*. But Sleiertin insists that Munch's painting was just one of many influences on the design. 'Pink Floyd's *The Wall* has some images that have a sort of similar look,' she said. 'And some of the old 1930s cartoons have characters with that type of appearance.' True, but Munch produced his painting in the late nineteenth century and it's been an icon of existentialist angst ever since then.

Finding the right mask still didn't solve all the problems concerning the killer's appearance. Craven realized they couldn't just have a killer in a mask without the audience being able to tell who it was by their clothes. 'We were trying to cast suspicion on a whole range of characters – teenagers and adults, males and females,' said Craven. 'So we had to conceive a costume that covered virtually every square inch of their bodies. We went through quite a bit of work with that to make sure it worked on screen.' The solution was a black gown which, together with the ghostface mask and hood, perfectly concealed the identity of the wearer.

Whether by design or a series of fortunate accidents, the completed costume became the perfect motif for the movie; with the white mask, the black hood and robe, the character symbolizes Death. But the mask itself undoubtedly owes much of its unsettling power to Edvard Munch's original image, a debt acknowledged, albeit unconsciously perhaps, by the producers with the very title they eventually gave the movie. Oddly enough, Craven was initially resistant to Miramax's decision to change Williamson's original title. 'We were incredibly fond of *Scary Movie*,' said Craven at the time, 'and at first we were upset they were going to change it, but we've come round to thinking that *Scream* is a pretty good title.'

One of the final tasks was to find a suitable composer for the movie. Craven's assistant, Julie Plec, came across Marco Beltrami's name on the Internet. Beltrami sent in a CD of his work which really impressed Craven and the others. The composer had only worked in TV before and had never scored a feature film, but Craven decided to go with him. 'I have a feeling he's going to deliver something unique and terrific,' said Craven at the time. And Beltrami's score certainly fitted, and enhanced, *Scream* just perfectly (he's subsequently worked on *Scream*s 2 and 3).

When Craven had a rough cut of the film ready, he screened it for Bob Weinstein, his brother Harvey and other Miramax executives.

They all reacted very positively to the movie, much to Craven's relief. And when there was an equally good reaction from a preview audience in New Jersey, Miramax told Craven, 'No changes. Just go finish it.' So pleased with the result were Miramax, they offered Craven a two-picture deal, provided he agreed to make the sequel to *Scream*. Craven happily accepted the offer, though taking care to stipulate that Miramax allow him to base one of the films on a non-horror subject (which he did three years later, making *Music of the Heart*).

But the actual release of *Scream* was still to come. Williamson exuded confidence: 'It's better than I envisioned it. I never knew how it was going to feel once it was shot, but Wes has got it. It's perverse, it's unsettling. Even in the comedic scenes you're on edge, you're uncomfortable... it's really unnerving.' Craven, however, was a little more wary about its prospects. He told *Fangoria* magazine just prior to the film's release, 'I'm holding my breath, you know. I rely on the expertise and the genius of Bob Weinstein, who has a knack for marketing things. It is a very, very competitive time and we're all... I wouldn't say *worried* but we're holding our breath. The stars certainly won't hurt. Whether their heat will work in this particular season or whether we'll be buried under *Beavis and Butt-head*, who knows?'

One of the earliest reviews of the film appeared in the trade weekly *Variety* on 16 December 1996, and it wasn't too reassuring:

> *Director Wes Craven is on familiar turf with his latest thriller,* Scream. *The setting is a small town, the protagonists are teens and there's a psychotic killer on the prowl. But he may have gone to the trough once too often, attempting an uneasy balance of genre convention and sophisticated parody. The pic's chills are top-notch, but its underlying mockish tone won't please die-hard fans. That adds up to no more than modest commercial returns and fast theatrical play-off... There's no question that the film-maker knows how to put an audience on the edge of its seat. But this yarn isn't content with visceral delight, and its attempts to instil irony and social perspective just slow down the proceedings.* Scream *is*

an interesting stab at altering the shape of horror. But it's one experiment that needed more lab time before venturing into the market-place.

The reaction from other reviewers was much more up-beat. Typical was this review in *Starburst* magazine:

Gleefully exploring the relationship between gore movies and their core audience, Craven's spoof horror, Scream, *generates plenty of knowing laughs while still managing to subversively thrill and cleverly chill. In much the same way that he breathed new life into his own* Nightmare on Elm Street *series last time out, Craven intelligently reinvents the slasher genre, and pays homage to it at the same time, courtesy of fan boy Kevin Williamson's stupendously elaborate script which manages to keep things scary even when the sinister events are at their funniest... This is the best time to be had in Horror cinema in years and I'm jealous of everyone who sees it for the first time. An instant classic.* Scream *reigns supreme.*

The *Variety* reviewer was also soon to be proven wrong on his predictions of how *Scream* would perform at the box office. Very wrong indeed. The Weinsteins were hoping for the movie to gross at least $20 million, which would have more than covered the film's production and advertising costs. Anything more than that would be cream on the cake. Craven himself thought that at the very best it might just reach the $30 million mark. 'That would have been just fine because no other film of mine had ever taken anything over $20 million.' On its release *Scream* did okay at first at the box office, taking $6.3 million over the weekend from 20 December 1996, but was far from looking like a financial blockbuster. And then a strange thing happened. Instead of peaking in its first week and then gradually falling away, the movie *increased* its weekly box-office takings in the following weeks: the take for the third week was over $10 million and it was still going up. Good reviews had helped, but it was the favourable word of mouth that ensured the film's growing popularity. Not only that but the 'repeat viewing' factor was also of importance. People were returning to see *Scream* not only for a second time, but for a third and fourth time – and bringing their friends. This caught the cinema owners by surprise as they'd only booked the film in for a normal run. As a result they were obliged, bizarrely, to take this money-spinner out of their cinemas for a brief period while alternative plans were hastily made. When *Scream* was re-released in April 1997 the box-office take continued to grow and by June it had grossed over $100 million.

Wes Craven and Kevin Williamson, not to mention the Weinstein brothers, were naturally overjoyed. And the scene was set for *Scream 2*.

SCREAM
THE GORE, THE CENSORS AND THE BACKLASH

Wes Craven had been having difficulties with the film censors throughout most of his career, starting with his first horror movie, *Last House on the Left*, which is still banned in the UK. In America his battles had been with the MPAA (the Motion Picture Association of America), the American equivalent of the BBFC (the British Board of Film Classification – formerly 'the British Board of Film Censors', a much more accurate title). While the MPAA had approved the release of *Last House*, albeit with cuts, Craven's relationship with the body had been a rocky one ever since. So much so that Craven's initial hesitation to accept the *Scream* assignment stemmed in part from his reluctance to become embroiled in yet another long series of arguments with the MPAA in order to secure the necessary R rating.

In its original form, Williamson's script was much gorier than the later versions and Craven could see that there would be problems. Even so, once he'd committed to the movie, Craven felt that a certain amount of gore was necessary if *Scream* was going to have the desired impact on audiences. According to Williamson, 'In the first draft I had the line, "The insides are slowly rolling down her leg", and stuff like that. But my agent said, "Take that out. You'll never sell it with that stuff in it." So I went back and excised all of the big gore. But when Wes came on board, we got to put it all back in.'

During the shooting of *Scream* the gore factor certainly sounded over the top. In charge of the blood was effects man Howard Berger of the KNB EFX Group, who had worked with Craven on three of his previous films, *People Under the Stairs*, *Vampire in Brooklyn* and *Wes Craven's New Nightmare*. Berger, interviewed on the set of *Scream* by *Fangoria* magazine, gave the impression of being someone who really enjoyed his work. He described with relish the state of Casey's boyfriend Steve after he's been attacked in the opening sequence of the film: 'She sees her boyfriend tied to a chair, completely gutted. He's still alive and his guts are hanging out. We created a lot of guts for this movie. Sometimes we use the real thing, like pig guts. I don't like to do that because I don't like handling them. So here we used rubber guts and hot-melt vinyl guts.'

For the scene where Casey's eviscerated body is found by her parents, hanging from a garden swing, an even gorier set-up was created by Berger. 'I wanted to do something different. We originally talked about just appliances or whatever but I didn't want to go that route. The victim is pretty much held together by her spine, gutted from breasts to belly-button. I wanted it to be completely carved out and you just see her spine holding her lower half to her upper half, so we used a full-body dummy. But I heard that in the rough cut it was taken out because it's so gory. We had tons of guts streaming down into a big steaming pile beneath her.'

Craven himself seems to have enjoyed shooting the gore scenes, as did the cast. 'We've all had a great time doing this. In the final scenes, everybody is covered in blood, and there was just this sense of hilarity on the set. I thought the cast would be resistant to doing this but it turned out I could hardly hold them back. I think it was because it was such a challenge for them, such a wild release of emotions. It is something that is so forbidden, you just can't believe you're seeing it. Audiences aren't used to seeing this, and it's just appalling... Anytime you're dealing with blood, it's like a nightmare technically, because it's horrendous dealing with the continuity. If you want to do a second take, it's off to the wardrobe to have the actors changed back to the way they were before. We even had special drip areas where the actors could stand so they wouldn't drip blood all over the set dressings.'

But the people at the MPAA failed to see the joke. Not surprisingly, they did insist on further cuts, particularly in the evisceration scenes. (The BBFC cut it even more for UK consumption, the video version being trimmed even more than the theatrical one, as is the usual custom.) Craven was annoyed: 'We had a shot where the guts fall out and then they're at rest but the MPAA said, "You cannot have any movement of the innards." So we had to use just the part where they're already out.' They objected to moments throughout the film but the worst objections concerned the intense ending, as Craven explains:

The MPAA flatly announced, 'You're miles from it. You'll probably never get an R rating.' Well, we did, but it took endless screaming and crying and writing letters and paring it back somewhat. None of the viewers at the test screenings complained that it was too gory. They all said, 'This is hilariously funny', or 'brilliant'. But the MPAA was just hysterical about it. They really made my life hell. They didn't respond to any letters I wrote, or to any comparisons I made to other films. I mean, they gave Romeo and Juliet *a PG-13, and that's just filled with kids and guns. Where is the consistent standard here? It's just impossible to find any consistency in their decisions.*

I think they're troubled by things that involve young people in real situations. It's ironic that they're perfectly comfortable with big Rambo-esque violence; that's fine because they don't see it as imitatable. I see that as really cheapening human suffering, because it makes [it] all like a cartoon. But with someone being stabbed in a kitchen or something, it's like, 'Oh my God, teenagers are going to pick up a knife and try and do that themselves!' It's really an insult to teenagers. The whole issue of violence in horror films is so false. There's so much real-life violence that kids have to deal with – to suggest that movies are creating that violence is just ridiculous. Films have only been around for 100 years, but you can look at any page of human history and see over-whelming amounts of violence. You can go into any high school library and pull out the Bible or Shakespeare or 100 other books and find so much gore that, if you looked at any of them as a contemporary project, they'd say, 'This is terri-ble – we can't expose our children to that!'

Ironically, when *Scream* was released the fiercest attack on the movie came from a fellow film-maker, the British director Ken Russell. *Scream* won the top prize at the annual Gerardmer Festival in France in 1997 but Russell, who'd been a member of the Festival jury and voted against it, reacted by issuing a statement that was published in the London newspaper, the *Evening Standard*. '*Scream*', said Russell, 'was really disgusting and should be banned. It was sadistic. Unnecessary images of young girls with their stomachs split from top to bottom and their mothers watching. These are just commercial films geared to make money out of glorifying murder.' Russell did admit that *Scream* was 'clever and based on horror film buffs. It could have been amusing, but it did not need the gore.' Considering that Russell directed such controversial films as *The Devils*, *Crimes of Passion* and *The Lair of the White Worm*, this crit-icism does seem somewhat surprising, but he maintained that, 'My stuff is not in this genre. There has been a shift to sadism and every director in America seems to have to go one step further.' He cited, predictably at the time, *Natural Born Killers* and *Pulp Fiction* to support this theory.

Williamson and Craven had briefly touched on the matter of cinema violence and its supposed influence on susceptible people in *Scream*, when they had the character of Billy, one of the killers, exclaim to Sidney that movies aren't to blame – they simply make psychos more creative. And in *Scream 2* they went further in addressing the matter, wittily and provocatively, within the context of the movie. However, events in the real world were to put the whole question of screen violence under even more intense scrutiny – and the *Scream* movies were implicated as a result.

SCREAM
STAR FILES

NEVE CAMPBELL THE QUEEN OF SCREAM

Describe Neve Campbell as the Queen of *Scream* to her face and you'd most likely receive a chilly response, if not worse. It is surely every young actor's dream to be the star of a hit movie. At the very least your status in the film industry immediately shoots upwards, along with the price your agent can ask for your services from now on. But to be associated with a hit *horror* movie is a double-edged sword, as Jamie Lee Curtis discovered back in 1978 with *Halloween*. It can be very difficult to escape from the genre connections, which tend to overshadow all your other work, and Campbell, while undoubtedly grateful for the recognition and money that the first two *Screams* have brought her way, must be hoping that *Scream 3* will be her last outing as a horror star.

A native of Canada (she was born in Ontario in October 1973), Campbell trained as a ballet dancer, starting at the age of 6, before becoming an actor in her mid teens. She suffered a nervous breakdown at the age of 14 and left home at 15 to become an actor. In 1995 she married a fellow Canadian actor, Jeffrey Colt. The marriage lasted just 3 years. She dated her *Scream* co-star Matthew Lillard for a time and is currently romantically linked with John Cusack. After working in Canadian TV, she moved to Los Angeles in 1994 and almost immediately landed the role of Julia Salinger Holbrook in the pilot episode of the superior teen-soap TV series, *Party of Five*. The series, created and

produced by Chris Keyser and Amy Lippman for Columbia, was a big
success and served as a fine showcase for the young cast; Jennifer Love
Hewitt, a later addition to the series, followed in Campbell's footsteps
and appeared in the Kevin Williamson-scripted *I Know What You Did
Last Summer* and, unfortunately for her, its sequel.

Two years later and Campbell had a leading role in *The Craft*,
playing one of four teenage witches. This wasn't her first genre experience: she'd appeared in the Toronto stage production *The Phantom
of the Opera* and in a TV production of *The Canterville Ghost*. And
then, in the same year as *The Craft*, she got *the* leading role in
another genre movie – *Scream*.

During the making of *Scream*, Neve made all the right sounds to
interviewers. Of her character, Sidney, she said, 'What attracted me to
this part is that Sidney is a very strong and resilient character... She's
very alone within the film because she doesn't feel she can trust
anybody, not even her boyfriend. I also loved the fact that, although
my character is somewhat the victim to begin with, by the end she
becomes the heroine and gets very tough.' At this stage she was still
sounding positive about appearing in horror movies, though she
admitted she didn't like watching them herself. 'I'm one of those
people who are so terrified by them, I have to sit with a pillow in front
of my face. I can't watch them, but I love playing in them. *The Craft*
was similar to *Scream* because it was about four women who, as they
emerge from childhood, take power and control over their lives.'

She also enjoyed the actual making of the film. Like many of the
other cast members who were playing teenagers, Campbell was in
her early twenties and the shooting of *Scream* provided her with the
rare opportunity to socialize with actors her own age. She told
Empire magazine: 'We'd be covered in blood and go home at seven
in the morning after shooting all night and close all the curtains, to
pretend it was time for bed, open a bottle of wine and talk for hours.
We had so much fun. It was one of those groups that really clicked.'

And she had good things to say about Wes Craven:

*Wes is one of the best acting directors I've yet to work with.
Doing a TV series like* Party of Five, *I work with twenty-four*

directors in one season. There are some good ones, and others who are very technically oriented, who haven't a clue how to direct actors. But Wes is incredible in that area. He really creates images for you, to help you get to where you need to be within the scene. We were doing one scene and I'd done a few takes that weren't working right so Wes said to me, 'Okay, now imagine you've got a thousand bullets ringing through your body. Now go do it.' That kind of insight helped me a lot.

One imagines it would.

But after *Scream* was released it wasn't long before Campbell was having second thoughts about being associated with the biggest horror movie event in years. 'I don't want to get stuck in that genre,' she told an interviewer. 'Jamie Lee Curtis managed to break out and did quite well for herself, but I really don't want the comparison.' And she was already expressing her reluctance about appearing in the sequel: 'Miramax made sure we were all committed to the sequel before we finished shooting the first one. When I originally signed I agreed to do it because you don't think it'll happen.'

And after she'd shot *Scream 2* she was still sounding apprehensive about her situation, saying she wasn't sure if she would do the third film. 'I'm a little scared of that. I don't want people to think that *Scream* movies are all I can do. That's why I've really been trying to do other films as well... If I had a choice between *Scream 3* or some other role I love, I'd do the other role.'

As we know now, she did star in *Scream 3*, but she also made a few interesting movies between *2* and *3* as well. Her role in John McNaughton's twisty, and downright kinky, *Wild Things* (1998) directly contrasted to her straight-arrow Sidney character in the *Scream*s. In that, she played a trailer-trash type young woman who, along with Denise Richards, is apparently being exploited by a manipulative Matt Dillon, but in the end is revealed to be the real manipulator behind the murderous events. Playing a killer of ambiguous sexuality (a lesbian relationship between her character and Denise Richards is suggested) couldn't have done her career any harm at all.

Her role in her next film, *54*, about the famous Studio 54 discotheque, was a complete change of pace. She played a young 1970s TV soap star who appears to share certain characteristics with Campbell herself. The same year she co-produced, with her older brother, Christian, a low-budget Canadian art-house movie called *Hairshirt*. It's a romantic comedy in which she plays a spurned lover attempting to get revenge on her former boyfriend (L. Dean Ifill, who also directed under the name 'Dean Paras'). It has had little exposure but attracted good reviews at the time of its première at the 1998 Toronto Film Festival. (Trivia info-dump: Rebecca Gayheart, who had a small role in *Scream 2*, and featured in Kevin Williamson's *Wasteland* TV series, also has a small role in *Hairshirt*.) In 1999, before *Scream 3*, she made *Three to Tango*, another romantic comedy in which she co-starred with Matthew Perry from *Friends*, and then a thriller called *Drowning Mona*. Directed by Nick Gomez, it stars, along with Campbell, Bette Midler, Danny Devito, William Fichtner, Casey Affleck, and none other than Jamie Lee Curtis.

One imagines that Campbell and Curtis had a lot to talk about.

And what persuaded Campbell to return once more as Sidney in *Scream 3*? 'To be honest, I just felt that I owed it to fans of the first two. I was also given a nice little contract to do other films, so it's worked out well.'

COURTENEY COX
(A.K.A. Courteney Cox Arquette, A.K.A. Courteney Arquette)

It's odd, but the now traditional moment in the *Scream* movies when Neve Campbell's character, Sidney, punches Courteney Cox's Gale Weathers on the jaw, gets a disturbingly positive reaction from the audience. It may be just because Gale is an annoying character, but one suspects that the audience is also enjoying the sight of Monica from *Friends* having her lights punched out.

The TV series *Friends*, of course, is what gave Courteney Cox's career a much-needed upward push after an erratic ten-year trajectory. Born in Alabama in 1964, Cox studied architecture at college before moving to New York, where she became a model and also worked at a concert-booking agency. This was her introduction to show business and led to her appearing in the Bruce Springsteen music video *Dancing in the Dark* in 1984 (now much lampooned). That same year she got a part in the long-running daytime TV soap *As the World Turns* and continued to work in TV until her first movie role – in *Masters of the Universe* in 1987. Strangely enough, this didn't lead to bigger and better movie parts and it was back to TV for Courteney. She was, legend has it, the first person ever to say the word 'period' on American network TV. It was for a Tampax commercial. She did make other film appearances pre-*Scream*, most notably in *The Opposite Sex and How to Live with Them* in 1992, and in *Ace Ventura, Pet Detective* in 1994. But it was getting the part of Monica in *Friends* (she originally auditioned for the role of Rachel) in 1994 that really turned things around for her.

And then came *Scream*, of which she said at the time, 'This is a great movie. I'm really proud of it. And Wes is an amazing director, he really knows how to capture the thriller *and* horror aspects... It scared the shit out of me and I love good scary movies.' More recently she said of *Scream* and her role as Gale Weathers, 'I knew it was a safe choice. I didn't read anything else that made me feel, "Wow, I've got to get my teeth into this." I love the idea of playing a character that you love to hate. In *Scream 2* I was booed by the audience, which made me happy. If it was up to me, Gale would be bitchy from top to bottom and never be sweet.' Incidentally, her nickname 'CiCi' was also the nickname given to the character played by Sarah Michelle Gellar in the same film.

Apart from the three *Scream* films Courteney has also made *Commandments* (1997), *The Runner* (1999) and *The Shrink Is In* (1999). The latter also stars her husband, David Arquette, who she met on the first *Scream*, (prior to this she had a 6-year relationship with Michael Keaton). It is a romantic comedy directed by Richard Benjamin about 'a young woman who poses as a psychiatrist in order to win over her Prince Charming' and was co-produced by the husband and wife team. Sounds sweet, and no doubt a case of art imitating life.

DREW BARRYMORE

Though still only 24 years old, Drew Barrymore already has a lengthy list of film credits an actor twice her age would be pleased to display. After becoming world famous at the age of 7 thanks to her role in *E.T.* and enjoying (if that's the right word) a prolific career as a child actress, she went spectacularly off the rails in her early teens and ended up in drug and alcohol rehabilitation programmes. She resumed her film career in 1992 in movies like *Poison Ivy* and *Gun Crazy*, but it wasn't until 1996 and her roles in Woody Allen's *Everyone Says I Love You* and *Scream* that she put herself back on the Hollywood map.

Though her part in *Scream* is a small one – she plays doomed Casey Becker in the prologue – it made a big impression. 'Most movies don't really scare me,' she told *Empire* magazine after making *Scream*, 'but the writing was so good in this, and Kevin Williamson had written me such a good scene – what did scare me as a kid was *When a Stranger Calls* and this was very much paying tribute to that – so there was no question in my mind that I wanted to do this.'

Her post-*Scream* movies include *The Wedding Singer* and *Never Been Kissed*, and she is currently planning to produce the big screen version of *Charlie's Angels*, starring herself, Cameron Diaz and Lucy Liu. But her credibility as a major Hollywood player is not helped by her continued predilection for taking her clothes off in public. After posing for *Playboy* in 1995, flashing David Letterman on his TV show and stripping at a nightclub in New York, she was recently photographed nude in a Beverly Hills car park. 'I was only changing clothes,' she said. 'I do it all the time. I mean, our skin is just a space-suit and what are clothes?'

Time for her godfather, Steven Spielberg, to act again: he once had his art department alter her nude photographs in a copy of the *Playboy* she'd appeared in so that she appeared fully clothed, then sent her the magazine with a note saying, 'Cover yourself up.'

MATTHEW LILLARD

Matthew Lillard stood out as Stuart Macher, one of the two killers in *Scream*. He gave a bravura performance, particularly in the final scenes, the high point of which comes when, after being stabbed several times and covered in blood, he discovers that Sidney has called the police and whimpers over the phone to her, 'My Mom and Dad are going to be *so* mad at me!'

Born in Michigan in 1970, Lillard's acting career began when he got a job as an extra in *Ghoulies 3* (1991). After moving to New York and attending the Circle in the Square drama school, he got his first big part in John Waters' *Serial Mom* in 1994. In 1995 he had a small role in *Mad Love* (which also featured Drew Barrymore and Liev Schreiber) and a bigger role in *Hackers*. Post-*Scream*, he had a large role in the teen comedy *She's All That* (1999), starred in the science fiction *Wing Commander* (1999) with Saffron Burrows, and had a leading role in Kenneth Branagh's all-singing, all-dancing version of Shakespeare's *Love's Labour's Lost* (1999).

Of working on the latter film he said, 'Ken never asked if I could sing. At some point I volunteered the fact that I could dance a little but I couldn't sing a lick. My fear was that he was going to hear me open my mouth and send me home.' With the dancing scenes it was the 'dance belt' that caused him some grief. 'It's the undergarment you have to wear. There's nothing like being in a full top hat and tails and having a dance belt run up your ass.'

SKEET ULRICH

Skeet Ulrich, who played the seriously sick Billy Loomis in *Scream*, is handicapped, career-wise, because he bears a strong resemblance to Johnny Depp. What's really spooky is that one of Depp's earliest roles was also in a Wes Craven movie, the first *A Nightmare on Elm Street*.

Ulrich had small roles in a few films prior to *Scream*, including *The Craft*, which had co-starred Neve Campbell, but it was his unsettling performance in *Scream* as one of the two psychopaths (and the one who treated poor Sidney very, very badly) that seemed to get him noticed. Curiously, he said of *Scream*, 'I don't really think of it as a horror film. To me, horror films are always about some escaped mental patient, or monster, or supernatural element, and this is about people you could run into on the street anywhere.' Yes, and if you do, it would be advisable to keep on running.

After *Scream*, Ulrich appeared in *The Newton Boys* (1998) and then turned down a role in *Armageddon* in order to marry his *Newton Boys* co-star, British actress Georgina Cates. After making the action-thriller *Chill Factor*, his latest film role is in the American Civil War epic *Ride with the Devil*, for which he received glowing reviews.

The 29-year-old actor hails from the same state as *Scream* writer Kevin Williamson, North Carolina, and has plans to become a producer. Presumably his main ambition is to have people say that Johnny Depp bears a striking resemblance to Skeet Ulrich.

ROSE McGOWAN

Rose McGowan's vivacious character Tatum in *Scream* stuck in the audience's memory for more reasons than one – she was fortunate enough to suffer the most ingenious death scene in the movie. She gets stuck in the doggy-flap of an electric garage door while trying to flee from the killer and then has her neck slowly broken against a ceiling beam when the killer activates the door. 'I have the coolest death in the movie,' she said at the time. 'I die in a doggy door, but not doggy-style.'

McGowan was born in Florence, Italy in 1975, and was raised there in a religious commune called the Children of God. She had only appeared in one previous movie, *Encino Man* (1992), when she was chosen by director Gregg Araki to play one of the leads in his 1995 indie production, the controversial *The Doom Generation*, in which her performance as a seriously zapped-out teenager attracted a lot of attention. Her *Scream* role followed the next year and since then her career has seen a steady climb (though she didn't have much to do in *Phantoms* except look understandably worried in Liev Schreiber's presence).

Her most recent movie is the black comedy *Jawbreaker* (1999), written and directed by Darren Stein. A superior high school movie that's been described as *Heathers* mixed with *Clueless* and *Carrie*, McGowan's performance as the ultra-bitch Courtney (!) has been highly praised (as was that of her co-star Rebecca Gayheart, who was in *Scream 2*, as well as being one of the stars of Kevin Williamson's *Wasteland* TV series). McGowan's fiancé, Marilyn Manson, was also in *Jawbreaker* and of their sex scene together she said, 'It's better than having to do a sex scene with someone you don't know. Like, "This is Bob, he's the one going to be pretending to have doggy-style sex with you."' At least in this doggy-related scene she doesn't get her neck broken.

SCREAM
THE PLOT

On the outskirts of the town of Woodsboro, high school student Casey and her boyfriend, Steve, are brutally butchered by a knife-wielding killer wearing a white ghost mask and a hooded black robe. Almost a year earlier, the mother of another Woodsboro high school student, Sidney Prescott, was raped and murdered, apparently by a local man, Cotton Weary, who was convicted of the crime and is currently on death row.

These new murders have put the town of Woodsboro into a state of fear, and attention is centred on the town's high school. At the school, Sidney, her boyfriend, Billy Loomis, and their fellow students, Tatum, Stuart and Randy, speculate on just who the killer might be. The murders have also attracted the attention of TV reporter Gale Weathers, who maintains that Cotton was innocent of the murder of Sidney's mother and has a forthcoming book backing up her theory.

That night Sidney, alone in the house – her father, Neil, being away on a business trip – first receives a threatening phone call and is then attacked by the masked killer, Ghostface. She eludes him, aided by his tendency to fall over the furniture while chasing her. Barricaded in her bedroom, she manages to call the police. Then Billy arrives through her bedroom window, but Sidney's relief is short-lived when he drops a mobile phone and she realizes he must be the killer. Deputy 'Dewey' Riley, Tatum's brother, arrives and Billy is arrested.

THE PLOT

On leaving the police station with Tatum and Dewey, Sidney is confronted by Gale Weathers and her cameraman, Kenny. Gale wants Sidney to admit she's wrong about Cotton being her mother's killer. Sidney, understandably under stress, reacts by punching Gale in the face.

While spending the night at Tatum and Deputy Dewey's parents' house, Sidney receives another phone call from the killer – which must mean that Billy, still under arrest at the station, is innocent. Or is he?

The next day, at the high school, Sidney is attacked in the women's toilets by Ghostface. She escapes unharmed but later the school principal, Mr Himbry, is stabbed to death in his office by Ghostface, though his murder remains undiscovered. Meanwhile, Deputy Dewey is informed by his boss, Sheriff Burke, who has imposed a town curfew, that the threatening phone calls have been traced to Sidney's father, Neil Prescott's cellphone. Prescott now becomes the chief suspect.

That night Sidney and Tatum, accompanied by Dewey, attend an impromptu party at Stuart's house. Gale Weathers and her cameraman, Kenny, also turn up in their outside broadcast van. Gale drops in on the party and hides a miniature TV camera in the sitting-room, linked to a monitor in the van (though it has a 30-second delay). Tatum goes down to the garage to fetch more drinks and is murdered by Ghostface.

Oblivious to Tatum's fate, Sidney goes with Billy to an upstairs bedroom and they make love. Downstairs, the other students are watching a video of *Halloween* and are in turn being watched by Gale and Kenny in the van. Then Gale accepts Dewey's invitation to go with him to investigate an abandoned car that's been spotted a short way down the road. The students then learn that Principal Himbry's body has been found hanging, gutted, from a goalpost on the school football field. They head off back to town, leaving Randy alone in front of the TV, and Sidney and Billy upstairs.

Gale and Dewey find the car, which belongs to Sidney's missing father. They hurry back towards the house. Meanwhile, in the bedroom, Ghostface appears and stabs Billy. A terrified Sidney escapes through an upstairs window, falls into the backyard and discovers Tatum's dead body. She runs to the TV van, where she and Kenny see, on the TV monitor, Ghostface appear behind Randy in the sitting-room.

Forgetting about the time delay, Kenny leaves the van to help Randy… and walks straight into Ghostface, who cuts his throat. Ghostface then stabs Sidney in the shoulder as she tries to escape. She makes it out of the van and runs off into the woods.

Gale and Dewey return to the house. While Gale heads for her van to call the police, Dewey enters the house, expecting to find Neil Prescott lurking there. Gale, finding Kenny gone, gets into the van and starts to call the police on her mobile phone when Randy suddenly appears at the window. She hits him on the head with the phone and starts the van's engine… and just then Kenny's body slides into view across the windshield, leaking copious amounts of blood. The van lurches forward. Gale, panicked, loses control and it crashes.

Sidney returns to the house in time to see Dewey emerge – with a knife in his back. He collapses just as Ghostface appears behind him in the doorway. Sidney tries to escape in the patrol car but Ghostface has the keys to the ignition. Sidney is almost trapped in the car but again escapes in the nick of time. She reaches Dewey's body and grabs his gun, but now Ghostface has disappeared.

And then Randy and Stuart suddenly show up, each accusing the other of being the killer. Sidney slams the front door in their faces. And then Billy, still alive, falls down the stairs. He asks her for the gun and opens the door. Randy rushes in alone… and Billy shoots him.

Billy then tells the understandably confused Sidney that the blood he's covered in is fake and he's unharmed. Then he lets Stuart into the house and the two of them reveal to Sidney that *they* are the killers. They even killed her mother and framed Cotton Weary the year before. Sidney receives another unpleasant surprise when her father is produced, bound and gagged. Their plan, after they kill Sidney, is to shoot her father and make it look like suicide, that way pinning all the murders on him.

But then Gale appears, brandishing Dewey's gun. However, she fails to remove the safety catch and Billy overpowers her, knocking her out. He's about to shoot her when Stuart notices that Sidney has vanished. As Billy hunts for her, Sidney takes him by surprise and stabs him, then kills Stuart by dropping a TV on his head. Randy makes yet another reappearance, but is attacked by Billy, who then tries to kill Sidney again. Gale also makes a reappearance, back in possession of the gun, but this time has cleverly remembered to switch the safety catch off. She shoots Billy. Sidney takes the gun and, when Billy makes his expected final comeback appearance, she shoots him in the head. This time he stays dead.

SCREAM
CREDITS

Director . . . . **Wes Craven**

Screenplay . . . . **Kevin Williamson**

Cinematographer . . . . **Mark Irwin**

Production Designer . . . . **Bruce Alan Miller**

Original Music . . . . **Marco Beltrami**

Producers . . . . **Cathy Konrad, Cary Woods**

Co-Producer . . . . **Dixie J. Capp**

Executive Co-Producer . . . . **Stuart M. Besser**

Executive Producers . . . . **Bob Weinstein**
Harvey Weinstein
Marianne Maddalena

CAST

Dwight 'Dewey' Riley . . . . David Arquette

Sidney Prescott . . . . Neve Campbell

Gale Weathers . . . . Courteney Cox

Randy Meeks . . . . Jamie Kennedy

Stuart Macher . . . . Matthew Lillard

Tatum Riley . . . . Rose McGowan

Billy Loomis . . . . Skeet Ulrich

Casey Becker . . . . Drew Barrymore

Cotton Weary . . . . Liev Schreiber

Kenny, the Cameraman . . . . W. Earl Brown

Sheriff Burke . . . . Joseph Whipp

Principal Himbry . . . . Henry Winkler (uncredited)

Reporter . . . . Linda Blair (uncredited)

Fred the Janitor . . . . Wes Craven (uncredited)

SCREAM 2

SCREAM 2
THE MOVIE

'Sequels suck,' says Randy during the film class sequence in *Scream 2*. This was a reprise of one of the lines spoken by Casey during her conversation with the mystery phone-caller in the *Scream* prologue. Responding to the caller's opinion that *Nightmare on Elm Street* was 'scary', she says, 'Well, the first one was but the rest sucked.' And that was the central challenge facing Wes Craven and Kevin Williamson when they were putting *Scream 2* together – to make a sequel that *didn't* suck.

The biggest hurdle that all makers of sequels to successful movies have to overcome is this: How do you repeat the formula that made the first film a hit with audiences while, at the same time, ringing enough changes to that formula to make it seem fresh and possibly even original? It's a problem that most sequel-makers in the past have failed to solve, as is made amusingly clear in the classroom sequence, where the film students, including Randy (Jamie Kennedy), CiCi (Sarah Michelle Gellar) and Mickey (Timothy Olyphant), debate movie sequels. Randy states that, by definition alone, sequels are inferior films, but Mickey says that many sequels have surpassed their originals. Challenged by CiCi to name one, Mickey gives *Aliens* as an example. 'Well, there's no accounting for taste,' says CiCi scornfully. Randy asks for other examples and Mickey then names *Terminator 2*. 'You've got a hard-on for Cameron,' sneers CiCi, adding that she's referring to James Cameron. After other students name films like *House II: The Second Story*, Mickey triumphantly comes up with *The Godfather Part II*. As one critic pointed out, this particular bunch of film students aren't exactly clued-up on their subject if *Godfather II* is the *last* example of a superior sequel that they can think of. But the fact remains that most sequels *are* inferior to the original movies. The list of examples is practically endless: *Jaws 2*, *Exorcist II*, *Die Hard 2*, *French Connection II*, and so on. In short, sequels usually *do* suck.

One reason for sequels being inferior to their predecessors is that the film-maker who produced the first film usually declines to become involved in the follow-up and lesser talents are invariably assigned to the task. As Peter Biskind writes in his book *Easy Riders, Raging Bulls*: 'To his credit, Spielberg resisted studio pressure to do a sequel to *Jaws*. Sequels were considered *déclassé*, and for all his commercial inclinations he was too much a child of the Seventies to sully his hands with an exclusively pecuniary enterprise. Of course, Universal went ahead without him and *Jaws 2* became the first example of a practice that would fly in the face of all that the new Hollywood stood for.' However, Francis Ford Coppola had been made an offer by Paramount he couldn't refuse (he needed the money) and so agreed, reluctantly, to make the sequel to his superb movie, *The Godfather*. In the end, *The Godfather Part II* turned out, to everyone's surprise, to be arguably superior to his first film.

It was this Coppola/*Godfather* factor that made the portents favourable for *Scream 2*'s chances of breaking the curse of the sequel, as both the director and writer of *Scream* had agreed to work on the second film. And Miramax backed them with a bigger budget, which at the very least ensured the return of the stars of the first film – Neve Campbell, Courteney Cox and David Arquette – along with enlisting some rising new young talent. The latter included Sarah Michelle Gellar (already a name because of the success of her *Buffy the Vampire Slayer* series on TV), Jerry O'Connell (from TV's *Sliders*), Jada Pinkett (from *The Nutty Professor*, as well as being Mrs Will Smith), Elise Neal (from TV's *SeaQuest DSV*) and Timothy Olyphant. Another new addition to the cast was veteran TV and film actress Laurie Metcalf (best known for playing Roseanne Barr's sister in the *Roseanne* TV series), while Liev Schreiber, who had the smallest of cameos in *Scream*, returned for a longer appearance as the former chief suspect, Cotton Weary.

Continuing with the key innovation of *Scream*, that of building the action around a scenario heavy with cinematic references and knowing in-jokes, Craven and Williamson hit upon the idea of starting *Scream 2* with a classic film-within-a-film set-up. (This was not new territory for Craven; he'd done something similar in *Wes Craven's New Nightmare* with its premise of having the real-life actors from *A Nightmare on Elm Street* play 'themselves' in a story centred around the making of another *Nightmare* movie.) In the prologue two college students are attending a sneak preview of *Stab*, which is based on TV reporter Gale Weathers' book, *The Woodsboro Murders*, about the 'true-life' series of murders that occurred in the town of Woodsboro. *Stab* is, of course, a remake of *Scream*. Neat as this idea is, one does have doubts that even the crassest of Hollywood producers would have the audacity, not to mention the sheer bad taste, to turn a book about a series of recent, real-life, horrendous killings into a blatant exploitation horror movie, but then again...

The fact that the two students, Maureen (Jada Pinkett) and Phil (Omar Epps), are black allows Craven and Williamson to compensate for a failing in *Scream*, and one they were criticized for: the film completely lacked any black characters. *Scream 2* redresses the balance by having a total of four black characters. As Maureen, who makes it clear that she'd prefer to see the new Sandra Bullock film playing down the street rather than sit through a horror movie, says to Phil, 'I'll tell you what it [*Stab*] is – it's a dumb-ass white movie about some dumb-ass white girls getting their white asses cut the fuck up.' She adds that the horror genre is famous for marginalizing black characters. As well as Maureen and Phil, the other two black characters in *Scream 2* are Sidney Prescott's room-mate, Hallie (Elise Neal), and Gale Weathers' new cameraman, Joel (Duane Martin). Later, after Joel has discovered the fate of Gale's previous cameraman (Joel: 'He was gutted.' Gale: 'He wasn't gutted, his throat was slashed. As with any job there are a few drawbacks.'), he gets to say to Gale: 'Brothers don't last long in situations like this.' (The scriptwriters of *Deep Blue Sea* shamelessly had one of their black characters come out with an almost identical version to Joel's last line.) However, Joel does make it through to the end in one piece, while Hallie most definitely doesn't. The killers' final score of victims in *Scream 2*: five white and three black. That's equality, of sorts.

When Maureen and Phil enter the cinema, which is full of people running about dressed as Ghostface from *Stab/Scream*, we get to see, on the cinema screen, parts of the prologue of *Stab*. This recreates some of the dialogue from *Scream* but has Heather Graham in Drew Barrymore's original role of Casey. Once again there is popcorn cooking on the stove while Casey discusses scary movies with her mystery phone-caller, but in a departure from *Scream*'s prologue there is now a scene where Casey prepares to take a shower – a dig at the type of teen-slasher movies that *Scream* was deconstructing, not to mention sending up.

Having Heather Graham play Drew Barrymore is a nice joke, and more fun is to be had with the casting of *Stab* later on in the movie when there's a cut to a TV in the college cafeteria and we see Tori Spelling, as herself, talking to an interviewer about her role as Sidney Prescott (Tori Spelling had been disparagingly referred to by Sidney in *Scream*). Randy complains to Dewey: 'I don't get it. They get Tori Spelling to play Sid and they get Joe Blow nobody to play me. At least *you* get David Schwimmer – I get the guy who drove Jane Seymour's coach in one episode of *Dr Quinn...*'

As with the original *Scream*, the prologue of *Scream 2* features the murder of a sympathetic female character. If anything, the murder of Maureen in the cinema is even more disturbing than the death of Casey in the first film. At least her boyfriend, Phil, dies quickly, if in somewhat unbelievable circumstances, when he is stabbed in the ear through a partition in a toilet cubicle (you've got to hand it to the killer for knowing when and exactly where Phil put his ear to the partition to listen more closely to the suggestive sounds coming from the adjacent cubicle). Maureen's death, however, is a much more prolonged affair. She is stabbed repeatedly by the masked killer as she tries to get away from him in the crowded auditorium (full marks to the sound technicians, Ivan Johnson and Joe Milner, for producing the most stomach-churning knife-blade-slicing-into-flesh sound effects since *Play Misty for Me*) before expiring slowly in front of the cinema screen – and a shocked audience that includes, disturbingly, a number of watching Ghostfaces.

The film's second murder also packs a punch, involving as it does Sarah Michelle Gellar. Her character, Casey 'CiCi' Cooper, is alone – supposedly – in a sorority house, and watching *Nosferatu* on TV, when Ghostface strikes. CiCi puts up a good fight (as in all the attack sequences in both films, Ghostface initially takes a lot of punishment from his victims, and is also prone to tripping over any item of household furnishing that happens to be in his way), but meets a messy end when she is finally trapped on an upstairs balcony, stabbed twice in the back and then thrown onto the stone patio below to her death. The scene carries a special *frisson* simply because CiCi has a lot in common with Gellar's Buffy persona and it comes as rather a shock to see 'Buffy' end up as a bloody corpse instead of kicking the killer's ass through the scenery. Interestingly, as it's later revealed that Mickey is one of the two Ghostface killers, it's likely that he chose CiCi as his victim simply because of her sneering remarks about his taste in movies in class – although this possible motive for her murder is never directly referred to...

But the later murder of Hallie, Sidney's room-mate, is effective as well, coming as it does after what is probably the film's most suspenseful sequence. When Ghostface takes over the police car carrying Sidney and Hallie and crashes it, the two young women must crawl over his apparently unconscious body in the front seat in order to climb out of the window. When the anticipated, and dreaded, springing-to-life moment doesn't occur and Sidney and Hallie escape unharmed from the car, Craven turns the screws by having Sidney insist on returning to the car to unmask Ghostface, while Hallie waits anxiously on the street corner. Except, of course, when Sidney looks into the car, Ghostface is gone... and seconds later appears behind Hallie and cuts her throat.

The murders in the cinema provide a handy device for Williamson and Craven to reunite the key members from the original movie – the ones who are still alive, that is. Sidney and Randy are already fellow drama students at Windsor College (the same college as the first two victims attended) and naturally, hard-nosed TV reporter Gale Weathers (Courteney Cox) is quickly on the scene. She has two good reasons for being there: apart from wanting to cover the story, she has a personal interest because the murders occurred during the screening of the movie based on her book. When we first see her in *Scream 2* she is talking to somebody on her cellphone and telling them excitedly that it would be stupid to cancel *Stab*'s release because of all the free publicity it's receiving. Then Dwight 'Dewey' Riley, now sporting a limp as a result of injuries suffered at the hands of the original killer, Billy Loomis, turns up on the campus. He's come because he's worried about Sidney, but his presence also provides the film-makers with another potential suspect to add to the already growing list. That list soon includes Sidney's new boyfriend Derek (Jerry O'Connell) and his friend Mickey, as well as Cotton Weary (Liev Schreiber), the man who was wrongly accused of killing Sid's mother and clearly someone with an axe to grind.

Another suspect is local newspaper reporter Debbie Salt who, declaring herself to be a big fan of Gale, is soon pestering the TV woman to the point of distraction. Unfortunately, the main reason why we automatically slot her into the suspect category is that she's played by Laurie Metcalf, an actress with a high profile, thanks to her film and TV roles. One automatically knows she wouldn't be in the movie simply to play a minor role as a bothersome reporter – she might as well be carrying a neon sign saying 'Surprise Killer'. It's a pity that Randy, in his list of horror film rules, didn't include the one that says: Always be suspicious of a big-name guest star in an apparently minor role.

Randy *does* deliver a revised version of his rules of horror films from the original *Scream*. In the college cafeteria, when he's discussing the new murders with Dewey, he outlines the rules of a sequel: 'Number One, the murder count is always bigger. Number Two, the death scenes are always more elaborate, more blood, more gore – *carnage candy* – your core audience always expects it. And Number Three, if you want your sequel to become a franchise, never *ever*—'

Alas, we never find out what Number Three is because Dewey interrupts to ask how they're going to find the killer. Randy then proceeds to run through the likely suspects, which includes Sidney's boyfriend Derek, but dismisses him for being too obvious. He also considers Mickey, who he describes as a freaky Tarantino film student – a category he understandably puts himself into. Dewey says that that makes *him* an ideal suspect...

Randy agrees, but points out that if he's a suspect, so too is Dewey. Then he raises Hallie's name as another possible contender. Dewey points out that serial killers are typically white males but Randy says, 'That's why it's perfect. It's sort of against the rules but not really. He mentions Mrs Voorhees, the murderer in *Friday the 13th*, as a perfect example of a surprise serial killer. Then Randy suggests Gale Weathers as a candidate. Dewey is doubtful but Randy suggests that's only because he's sweet on her. And when Dewey tries to deny it, Randy says, 'Please, this is *me* talking. Randy, the unrequited love slave of Sidney Prescott. I know all about obsession.'

Unfortunately, *Scream 2* was to mark the last appearance of the entertaining Randy (and Jamie Kennedy). The next day, while discussing the situation with Dewey and Gale on the campus lawn (this scene contains the second of the film's two *Friends* in-jokes: when Gale lights up a cigarette Dewey asks when she started smoking. Randy says it was since nude pictures of her appeared on the Internet. Gale protests that they only used her head in the pictures – the body was Jennifer Aniston's), Randy gets a call from the killer. While Dewey and Gale go off looking for anyone who looks suspicious, using a mobile phone in the vicinity, Randy carries on a conversation with the killer in an attempt to keep him on the line. When the caller asks him, as usual, what his favourite movie is, Randy says it's *Showgirls*. Then the killer gets personal, telling him he's never going to be the leading man and that he'll never get the girl... Which turns out to be true, because shortly after Randy has told the killer that his predecessor, Billy Loomis, was a homo-repressed mother's boy, he is dragged into Gale's OB van and diced and sliced to death by Ghostface. (If Ghostface is, at this point,

Billy's mother, then the motive for her killing Randy is obvious, but if it's Mickey under the mask, then his motive might be the same as the one for his killing of CiCi – he took offence at having his taste in movies mocked by Randy during the film class sequence.)

This development not only means the end of Randy as a character but also removes him from the list of possible suspects, which is a shame. As it turns out, the climax doesn't offer much in the way of surprises, unlike the first film. Williamson does perform a sleight-of-hand towards the end, which seems to confirm Sidney's suspicions about her new boyfriend, Derek, but this is quickly proved incorrect when Mickey, after revealing himself as the killer, shoots Derek dead. 'I'm sorry,' Sidney tells Derek as she vainly tries to stem the blood flowing from the bullet hole in his chest, but by then it's rather too late for apologies. Once again, poor Sidney's love life has gone abruptly down the tubes.

As for Mickey's motives for becoming a serial killer, they are far from solid – or even very clear. When Sidney accuses him of being sick, like Billy Loomis, Mickey claims that he's entirely different from Billy. Whereas Billy was trying to get away with murder, Mickey *wants* to get caught! He even has his defence planned out. In a nice conceit by Williamson, Mickey intends to blame the movies at his trial. 'Can't you see it? The effects of cinema violence on society. I'll get Bob Dole on the witness stand in my defence... Hell, the Christian Coalition will probably pay my legal fees. It's airtight, Sid.' Of course, Williamson and Craven are less interested in providing Mickey with a believable motive than in having another go at the American film censorship lobby, not to mention the Republican Presidential candidate Bob Dole who, at the time when Williamson was writing his script for *Scream*, unleashed an attack on Hollywood and the violence contained in movies such as *Natural Born Killers* (a bandwagon that President Clinton subsequently climbed on board, following the Columbine school massacre).

Earlier in *Scream 2*, during the film class sequence, Williamson and Craven have the students debating the same issue after their teacher, referring to the murders at the film preview of *Stab*, says that what happened to the two murdered students was a direct result of the type of movie they went to see. CiCi (soon, of course, to become a victim herself) reacts angrily, saying, 'That's so moral majority! You can't blame real-life violence on entertainment.' But other students disagree; one points out that the killer was wearing the same mask as the killer in the movie, therefore the film was directly responsible. CiCi refuses to accept this and insists that movies are not responsible for anyone's actions. Randy backs her up, saying, 'Life is life. It doesn't imitate anything.' It is clear here which of the characters is voicing the heartfelt opinions of the film-makers...

As expected, Debbie Salt makes an appearance in the climax, gun in hand, with Gale Weathers as her captive (at this point Gale has just narrowly escaped from Ghostface, having witnessed Dewey being apparently hacked to death). 'Mrs Loomis!' exclaims Mickey in triumph. 'Billy's mother. Nice twist, eh, Sid? You didn't see it coming.' Well, Sidney may not have seen it coming but viewers who know their horror films, or at least are familiar with the first *Scream*, wouldn't have been too surprised at this development. The idea of a vengeful mother being the killer is lifted straight from *Friday the 13th*, as Randy had conveniently reminded us earlier. Even so, its use here does have a certain satisfying symmetry, seeing as it was getting the question wrong about the identity of the killer in *Friday the 13th* that led to the death of Casey and her boyfriend at the very start of the original *Scream*.

Mrs Loomis and Mickey have been working together, having met through the Internet on the 'psycho website'. But Mickey doesn't get to have his day in court – he is shot by Mrs Loomis who then says to Sidney, 'Mickey was a good boy but, my God, that "blame it on the movies" motive!... Poor boy was out of his mind.'

Some extra, much-needed tension is generated by the last-minute arrival of Cotton Weary, armed with a gun, just as Mrs Loomis is about to stab Sidney to death. There is a drawn-out moment of 'will he or won't he?' as Mrs Loomis, with a knife at Sidney's throat, tries to persuade him to let her kill Sidney. With her dead, he'll be the media star. As it's already been established that Cotton is somewhat unstable and only interested in selling his story to TV, and had earlier had his media proposition rebuffed by Sidney, it's just possible he may ally himself with Mrs Loomis. As he says to Sidney, at this point she must be having second thoughts about not taking up his offer to appear on TV with him...

After a long pause, Sidney tells him, 'Consider it done.' And Cotton promptly shoots Mrs Loomis.

There is the expected, and traditional, last-minute surprise. As Gale and Sidney peer warily at the prone Mrs Loomis, Gale asks if she's dead and Sidney replies that she doesn't know but that they always come back. Sidney and Gale shoot him in unison – several times. And then Sidney goes and coldly shoots Mrs Loomis in the forehead. 'Just in case,' she tells the others.

Probably the biggest surprise comes almost at the very end when we see that Dewey, against all the odds, is still alive. Considering the ferocity of the attack he endured earlier, and what appeared to be a definitive death scene by the actor, it does seem very unlikely. Perhaps it was written into his contract...

The film ends with the triumphant Cotton surrounded by eager reporters. He won't divulge what happened because he intends to sell his story to the highest bidder, but he will tell them one thing – that the story will make one hell of a movie.

So how does *Scream 2* compare to the first film? Pretty favourably overall (and some critics and fans preferred it to the first one). Despite the disadvantage of not possessing the novelty value of *Scream*, it delivers the goods on most levels and is again a satisfying blend of suspense, thrills and humour. While it may not actually be better than the first film, one thing is for sure – it definitely doesn't suck.

SCREAM 2
BEHIND THE SCENES

Scream 2 began shooting in Atlanta on 16 June 1997. At one point it was going to be called either *Scream Again* or *Scream Louder* before someone at Miramax came to their senses and settled for *Scream 2*. Wes Craven had a bigger budget, at least on paper – $23 million compared to the original film's $14 million – but with increased payments to all the principal players, both behind and in front of the camera, in real terms the budget was about the same. And the shooting schedule was just as tight as before, if not even tighter. Miramax wanted to get *Scream 2* into the cinemas by mid-December, releasing it on the same pre-Christmas date as the original *Scream* (which was still playing in many cinemas when *Scream 2* started filming). This meant that Craven, cast and crew had to work under a great deal of pressure to reach the deadline.

Another of Craven's problems involved the screenplay. Since the success of *Scream*, Kevin Williamson had been making up for lost time by committing himself to a variety of other projects, and his script for *Scream 2* was still incomplete when shooting was due to begin. As Craven told *Fangoria* magazine:

> *There was a lot of collaboration and a good many lines were improvised on the set... but I don't want to get into anything*

that might be upsetting to Kevin. But because it started very late, there was a lot of work on the scenes. Some of them were very, very thoroughly worked out by Kevin, and other things came in a very preliminary shape and were heavily worked on and improvised. Some of Duane Martin's [Joel, Gale's black cameraman] funny lines were his own.

But it was a difficult shoot for Craven. 'It was much tougher than the last one. There was very little time for mistakes and reshoots. We lost a whole day due to damage to the negative in Georgia, and there were a lot of what I call "technical reversals". We've had to go fast, it's been difficult physically and I didn't get much sleep.' Clearly there was some slight degree of tension between Craven and Williamson this time round, though in statements issued for public consumption both projected a picture of mutual harmony. However, even in interviews, the strain in the relationship showed through. Said Craven during one interview, 'I don't know what Kevin's feelings are about it, but frankly, you can't concern yourself about it at this point. You can't worry about anybody's feelings. You have to do what's best for the film. My feeling was that after we had a test screening Kevin came away very happy with the result. I assume he's generally happy with what I did. I *hope* he's happy.' But as *Fangoria* magazine pointed out, though Williamson was pleased overall with the finished film, he'd made it plain that he thought the film was too long and, if he'd had the right, he'd have removed certain scenes. According to Craven, 'Kevin wanted to cut out the entire library scene [where Sidney receives the death threat on her computer, and is then intimidated by Cotton Weary]. I also believe he was one of the people who wanted to cut the scene between Courteney and Duane at the van ["Brothers don't last long in situations like this"]. My feeling was that after we'd put it all together and saw it with an audience, we shouldn't cut anything. But I don't know what else, Kevin, in his heart of hearts, would have cut out.'

Craven himself was more than pleased with the finished film, despite its sequel stigma. '*Scream 2* actually feels more like the element of a trilogy rather than sequel. I'm proud to have been a part of this, whereas I wouldn't have been proud to be a part of

A Nightmare on Elm Street 2.' One factor that put the whole enter-prise at risk at an early stage was Neve Campbell's initial reluctance to appear in *Scream 2*. Everyone had agreed that her performance in the first film had been a major asset to the production. Though it was an ensemble acting piece, her character was definitely the lynch-pin on which the film depended for the story to work. A lesser actor in the role – one who couldn't carry the burden of being the centre of the action – would have seriously damaged the film. Therefore it was vital to the makers that she return for the sequel. And even though she was under contract with Miramax from the start to do two films, that was no guarantee she could be pressured into playing Sidney again if she didn't want to. 'I was nervous and apprehensive about doing the sequel,' she said, 'but only because the very reason a sequel is ever made is that the original film is so good. So it's a huge challenge to make a sequel as good as the first film. But I was extremely happy when I got the *Scream 2* script and realized that Kevin had carried that through-line of being able to laugh at oneself. That's what I thought made the first film so unique.'

Williamson had also taken care to add a little something to the role of Sidney in *Scream 2* that couldn't fail to appeal to Campbell: Sidney was now a college drama student. The sequences involving the rehearsals for the Greek play must have been an attraction for the actress, not the least being the scene where she has the opportu-nity to deliver a showy emotional breakdown on stage after seeing the killer lurking among the members of the masked chorus. (It also provided British actor David Warner with an effective cameo as her tutor.) No doubt it reminded her of her own background (Campbell originally trained as a dancer before taking up acting as a student, and her father is a drama teacher), though presumably she was never chased about on stage by a knife-wielding psycho during a dress rehearsal.

Craven sang her praises when the film was completed: 'Neve continues to amaze me. She's so powerful. Even though I saw it day after day in the dailies, the cumulative effect of her performance is just even more so. You're struck by her charisma. It doesn't hit you over the head, but it's one of those long-lasting strengths. She looks good and powerful and intelligent. She's got incredible control of her emotions. That's an amazing thing to watch.'

The new additions to the *Scream* stock company of actors were of a uniformly high calibre. As Kevin Williamson pointed out, 'We had people come in and audition for the film who don't usually audition.' Craven agreed: 'Everybody wanted to be in the sequel. We were able to cast bit parts with big stars.' And among the relative newcomers, Jada Pinkett in particular gives a memorable performance in her relatively brief role as victim number two, and her death scene in the cinema is especially affecting. 'Most of us younger actors in *Scream 2* were around 14 when *Nightmare* came out,' said Pinkett. 'That makes Wes, like, a total hero.'

One new problem the makers had with *Scream 2* was keeping the plot a secret until its actual release. 'It wasn't this bad on the first *Scream*,' said Craven, 'because people thought it was just another horror film. Now, suddenly, we have a movie that everybody, not just the horror genre people, are interested in. That tends to change things.' All the *Scream 2* cast members had to sign legal papers promising they wouldn't divulge anything about the screenplay, and the film was shot under conditions of heavy security. As part of the secrecy, the last 10 pages of the script were apparently printed on a special dark red paper that couldn't be photocopied or scanned, though this has the ring of a story generated by the publicity department. Despite all the precautions, 40 pages of the screenplay were posted on the Internet in the spring of 1997. This prompted Craven to issue a statement on the Internet claiming that, though the copy of the script was genuine, it was an early draft and major changes had been made to it during shooting. Especially to the ending, he stressed.

Backed by a $15 million advertising campaign from Miramax, *Scream 2* opened on schedule in mid-December 1997 at almost 3,000 cinemas across America. It attracted both glowing reviews and big audience figures, grossing over $32 million during the first three-day weekend. By the end of January 1998 it had reached $100 million. Discussions immediately began between Miramax and the *Scream* creative team about *Scream 3*, but it turned out that the process making the third film wouldn't be so smooth.

SCREAM 2
THE SECOND BACKLASH

It's ironic that, considering one of central themes of *Scream 2* is that movies don't influence real-life acts of violence (a conviction firmly held by both Wes Craven and Kevin Williamson), the *Scream* movies have been accused of doing just that.

On its release, *Scream* was accused of being the inspiration for a series of child murders in Japan. Following the discovery of the decapitated body of an 11-year-old boy, and two further attacks on 10-year-old girls, the Japanese police linked the murders to the influence of 'splatter movies', and for some reason *Scream* was singled out as the prime example. This was odd, as *Scream* hadn't been released in Japan. As Miramax's head of international marketing said, in spring 1997, 'No one in Japan has even seen *Scream* yet so there's no way it can be an influence.' Even so, on the advice of local distributors, Miramax cancelled the planned June release of the film in Japan.

Then, after the release of *Scream 2*, a Californian woman was stabbed to death in mid-January 1998, allegedly by her 16-year-old son and his 14-year-old cousin. After they were arrested by the police, the two boys claimed that they got the idea of murdering her from the *Scream* movies. According to the police, the boys had also intended to wear 'grim reaper' style costumes and use distorting voice-boxes like the killers in the movies, but they couldn't afford them. 'We think the movies are behind it,' said a police spokesman. Miramax issued a statement saying that the company was 'saddened by the tragic death'; Craven refused to comment.

In the UK the *Scream* films have been named by the police and the courts as the likely influence on at least two cases involving stabbings. The most recent case was in 1999, when two teenage boys, aged 14 and 15, were convicted of the attempted murder of a third teenage boy. It was claimed in court that the two carried out the knife attack only hours after watching *Scream*. The police also found drawings of the mask worn by the killer in the film in one of the boys' schoolbooks, along with drawings of knives. Predictably, the media – especially the tabloids – fastened onto the alleged link with *Scream*, whereas the fact that both boys had behavioural difficulties which, according to the judge, enabled a Harrogate drug-dealer to 'exercise undue influence over them' (the drug-dealer had exposed them to drugs, knives and black magic over a period of time at his home) somehow didn't receive the same amount of coverage.

The idea that a specific film can be directly responsible for some horrific act of violence has long been popular with law-enforcement agencies, certain journalists and politicians. The appeal of such a simplistic cause-and-effect explanation for otherwise inexplicable actions is obvious. It means that having to delve deeper into murky waters, where more complicated explanations lie, and where the true reasons may reflect unfavourably on the society involved, can be avoided. In Britain two high-profile examples, both of which justifiably shocked the UK, were the Hungerford massacre and the James Bulger murder. In the first, the movie *Rambo: First Blood* was almost immediately identified by the media as the culprit, simply because the killer wore a headband similar to the one worn by Sylvester Stallone in the film. And the movie *Child's Play 3* became, for a time, the convenient target in the latter case. Subsequent investigation found no evidence to support these supposed links in either case.

In America it was the massacre at the Columbine High School in the town of Littleton, near Denver, Colorado, that sparked off an unprecedented outbreak of Hollywood-bashing. No specific film was cited as the direct influence behind the young gunmen opening fire on their fellow students and teachers at the school; rather it was movies and TV as a whole – as well as video games – that got the blame. The moral panic spread quickly to the White House itself, where President Clinton insisted that Hollywood clean up its act or face restrictive legislation. (In the 1950s it was the comic book industry that became the politicians' scapegoat for the spread of juvenile delinquency; tough censorship laws were imposed and many comic-book publishing companies were forced out of business but without any discernible effect on the level of juvenile crime. In the late Fifties and early Sixties the moral spotlight moved on to television and movies and has tended to remain there ever since.)

America's powerful National Rifle Association was suspiciously eager to support this view, and its lobbyists quickly claimed that violent films and television, rather than guns, were the cause of violence. This is a pretty curious claim seeing that more than 40,000 Americans are killed in gun-related incidents every year. In 1997 17,566 people in America, most of them young men, killed themselves with a gun. And every day three Americans, on average, are killed *accidentally* by guns. It takes a brave politician or journalist to point out that the easy access to guns is the main factor in this slaughter.

Kevin Williamson stands by the line in *Scream*: 'Don't blame the movies, Sidney. Movies don't create psychos. Movies just make psychos more creative.' 'That sums it up in a nutshell,' said Williamson. 'I mean, some guy saw *Interview with a Vampire* and then drained all the blood out of his girlfriend's body. Something tells me he would have killed her anyway. He just happened to see the movie on the wrong night and it made him a little more creative, but that girl was already doomed. To blame the movies for that is just absurd.'

Wes Craven holds a similar position on the subject:

I could conceive that there could be a copycat killing where a killer, who is already completely nuts, might use a movie as his format or a pattern for a murder, but I think that person is going to kill anyway... If you're going to look at any single instance of something causing a death, then you'd have to eliminate 80% of the things in our society. People have been killed with pencils. We're killed all the time by cars and airplanes but we don't stop using them... the number of people getting killed by a copycat act is infinitesimally small, yet it's blown out of all proportion by the media. I think the reason why is that some people are interested in stopping the message, which is that there is madness in our society, there is violence that's out of control and unexamined. That's why certain people hate these horror films. They want us to sweep it under the carpet and act like everything is Disneyland, and it isn't.

But in the hysterical post-Columbine atmosphere, any movie or TV show that featured a combination of high schools and violence was a target. Episodes of *Buffy the Vampire Slayer* were pulled from the schedule, while a 1995 Leonardo DiCaprio movie *The Basketball Diaries*, an unsensational film about a high school basketball player and his battle with drugs, but which featured a dream sequence where the protagonist opens fire with a machine gun at his school, was heavily jumped on in retrospect. DiCaprio promised never to do it again.

It was just Kevin Williamson's sheer bad luck that his long-gestating labour of love, *Killing Mrs Tingle*, which he both wrote and directed, was about to be released. Based on a true incident from his high school days, it was about some students getting their revenge on a particularly obnoxious teacher, Mrs Tingle (Helen Mirren). Even changing the title to *Teaching Mrs Tingle* didn't appease the moral crusaders. Considering its subject matter, Williamson's film couldn't have been released at a worse time.

But with *Scream 3* Craven is adamant that they haven't let the present climate influence the movie. 'I don't think we're pulling back on the violence and gore,' he told *Fangoria* magazine towards the end of the picture's shooting schedule, 'but on the other hand I don't think we're exploiting it. I'm comfortable with the fact that the violence in *Scream 3* is real and appropriate. We're not pandering to the audience, but this is also not the *Reader's Digest* version of *Scream*, if that's what people are afraid of.' He later told another interviewer that they'd checked the script very carefully before shooting began to see if it looked like anyone in the movie was making violence seem cool. They were satisfied they were well within the bounds of a good murder-mystery and he also added drily that the script contained nothing that was 'going to incite any riots in public places.'

Craven, again with justification, thought that the spate of recent high school shootings in America, of which the Columbine incident was the most prominent example, had more to do with other causes – including the then-approaching millennium. 'It's a time period that, for certain people, especially the sort of loser elements in society, puts a lot of pressure on them. It suggests to them that extreme measures and actions are called for...' Craven cited a more recent incident where someone walked into a Baptist church in Texas and shot six people: 'There wasn't the slightest hint of him watching horror movies or anything like that. But nobody bothered to mention that. It's only when somebody brings up horror movies as an excuse that we're charged with causing all these things.'

STAR FILES

SARAH MICHELLE GELLAR

Everybody's favourite vampire slayer, Sarah Michelle Gellar, who came to a spectacularly sticky end in *Scream 2*, has been in show business since she started making TV commercials at the age of 4. In her early teens she progressed to dramatic roles, once playing the teenage Jackie Kennedy in a 1991 mini-series. Then in 1993 she joined the cast of *All My Children*, a long-running afternoon TV soap opera, produced in her home town of New York City, and stayed with the series for two years.

'It gave me an amazing understanding of the technical aspects of this industry,' said Gellar. 'How to hit a mark, how to not shadow somebody, how to play to the camera. And that way, when I got to night-time TV, all I had to do was worry about the performance. I learned so much just about being a professional on the set.'

At the age of 18 she moved to California and just over a year later had won the lead role in a new TV series – *Buffy the Vampire Slayer*. A mid-season replacement on the then new WB Network, and based on a not-very-successful 1992 feature film of the same name, expectations for the series were not high. Attending the press launch of the show at the Television Critics Association, Gellar and the other members of the cast had a grim experience when they went on stage to promote *Buffy*. 'We basically just sat there,' said Gellar.

'Nobody had any questions for us. We felt just horrible and were all in tears.'

Gellar was shooting *I Know What You Did Last Summer* (in which she died another messy death) in North Carolina when the first season of *Buffy* was aired. 'I was in this small town,' said Gellar, 'and I kept calling Warner Brothers, "How's the show doing? Did anybody watch it?" I had no concept...'

By then *Buffy* was well on the way to making her a star and since then Gellar has taken advantage of her new status by appearing in three feature films. Following a small but impressive role in *Scream 2*, she's starred in *Cruel Intentions* and *Simply Irresistible*.

Cruel Intentions is a super-cool and superior example of the teen movie genre (a teen version of *Dangerous Liaisons*), but Gellar would be well advised not to go the *Simply Irresistible* route again. In this she played a hapless chef who is befriended by a magic *crab*. Another career move like this and she might need to sharpen up a stake for her agent.

LAURIE METCALF

Before Laurie Metcalf endeared herself to horror fans by playing the villainous Mrs Loomis (a.k.a. fake reporter Debbie Salt) in *Scream 2*, she was best known as Jackie Harris, sister to Roseanne Barr in the long-running TV series *Roseanne*.

Born in Illinois in 1955, her acting background was in the theatre before she began appearing on TV and in films; she was an early member of the famous Steppenwolf Theatre Company of Chicago (John Malkovich was another). Her debut film role was in *Desperately Seeking Susan* in 1985, where she played the sister of Rosanna Arquette – who is, of course, the sister of her co-star in *Scream 2*, David Arquette. She displayed her talent for comedy with an amusing performance in the John Candy movie *Uncle Buck* in 1989, but is equally at home in straight dramatic roles such as the one in *Internal Affairs* in which she plays a policewoman alongside Richard Gere. Laurie has also appeared in such films as *Leaving Las Vegas*, *Bulworth* and *Runaway Bride*, as well as providing voices for both *Toy Story* and *Toy Story* 2. She has recently returned to TV comedy in the new American series, *Norm*.

LIEV SCHREIBER

Despite having a first name that computer spell-checkers keep wanting to turn into 'Live', Liev Schreiber is finally becoming a name that cinema-goers recognize, along with his distinctive features. His role as Cotton Weary in all three *Scream* movies is only partly responsible, but it certainly helped. Though he had roles in at least twelve movies before his brief appearance in *Scream*, including *Mad Love* (with *Scream* co-star Drew Barrymore) in 1995 and the highly regarded independent film, *The Daytrippers* (with *Scream 3* co-star Parker Posey) in 1996, Schreiber's work had been mainly in the theatre.

Born in California in 1967, Schreiberr was a drama graduate at Yale and ensures that he appears in an average of two plays a year despite his flourishing film career. A versatile and highly skilled actor, he nevertheless has the type of face – and the mannerisms when necessary – that makes him perfect for genre movies. His creepy performance in *Phantoms* in 1998 (with *Scream* co-star Rose McGowan) stands out – he's creepy even *before* he's possessed by the monster. He recently described how he got involved in the first *Scream* film:

> *I was doing Harold Pinter's* Moonlight *on Broadway. I was in hog heaven, but I was broke. And when they asked me to appear in* Scream *I waffled, because I really had issues with doing a horror movie. So I said I'd be in the movie if I didn't kill anybody, thinking they'd say forget it. But for the first* Scream, *literally, all I had to do was fly to Santa Rosa, stay in a first-class hotel and walk down some stairs for $10,000. So I said OK. Why not? It paid for all the Indie movies I love doing... In my wildest dreams I never thought I'd be in* Scream 3.

There are other perks to appearing in the *Scream* movies apart from the money: 'Here's the silly part. Before Courteney Cox married David Arquette, the *National Enquirer* ran this item, "Courteney's hot new stud, Liev Schreiber". Of course, it wasn't true, but I was thrilled.'

JADA PINKETT

Also known as Jada Pinkett Smith these days, as she's married to Will Smith, Jada Pinkett made a bloody splash in *Scream 2*, thanks to her graphic death in the film's pre-credits sequence. She was the one who was stabbed by Ghostface while attending the sneak premiere of *Stab* with her boyfriend – who also ended up dead.

Born in Baltimore in 1971, she started off in TV as a regular character in the series *A Different World* from 1991–93. She sprang to feature film prominence in *A Low Down Dirty Shame*, the 1994 comedy-thriller written and directed by Keenan Ivory Wayans, who also starred in it. Pinkett played Wayans' private eye hero's loyal assistant, Peaches Jordan, and got singled out by most reviewers as the film's chief asset. In 1995 she co-starred with Billy Zane in a horror movie, *Demon Knight*, and the following year co-starred with Eddie Murphy in *The Nutty Professor*. In 1997 came her role in *Scream 2*, of which she said: 'That was a really enjoyable experience. Wes Craven is such an exceptional talent. He let me do what I wanted to do. There were no restrictions. We never see really dramatic death scenes in horror movies and I wanted the chance to do one. I'm a big fan of horror movies.' After *Scream 2* came the lead role in the romantic comedy *Woo* (1998) and her latest film is Spike Lee's *Bamboozled*.

JAMIE KENNEDY

Jamie Kennedy made an impact as movie geek Randy Meeks in the first two *Scream* movies. He was the Quentin Tarantino sound-alike, who kept reminding the other characters of the rules – not to mention the dangers – of being in a horror movie.

Born in Pennsylvania in 1970, he started out as a stand-up comedian before numerous guest roles in TV shows led to him getting small parts in feature films, starting with *Romeo and Juliet* in 1996. *Scream* followed the same year and, apart from *Scream 2* in 1997, he's also appeared in *As Good as It Gets* (1997), *Starstruck* (1998) and *Enemy of the State* (1998). In 1999 he appeared in four films, including *Three Kings* with George Clooney and *Bowfinger* with Steve Martin and Eddie Murphy. Jamie has such a fervent following that there was speculation among his fans on the Internet that his character, Randy, despite being killed off in *Scream 2*, would somehow make a return in *Scream 3* – possibly in the form of a video message from beyond the grave – their hunch turned out to be well-founded.

SCREAM 2
THE PLOT

Maureen and Phil, two college students, are attending a sneak preview of the horror movie *Stab*, which is based on a book by TV reporter Gale Weathers, called *The Woodsboro Murders*. The cinema is full of people wearing the white ghost masks and black robes worn by the killer in the movie. When Phil makes a visit to the toilet he is stabbed in the ear through the cubicle wall. Wearing Phil's jacket, and a *Stab* mask, the killer takes the empty seat next to Maureen. Grabbing him during a scary moment in the movie, Maureen discovers her hands are covered in blood. The killer then stabs her to death...

Sidney Prescott, now a drama student at Windsor College, is alarmed when she hears of the murder of two of her fellow students. That the murders occurred during the screening of a movie based on events in her life suggests that there might be a connection. The reporters, waiting for her outside her college residence, have made the same connection. As has Gale Weathers, who arrives at the campus in the hope of talking to Sidney, only to find herself being pestered by reporter Debbie Salt, who writes for a local newspaper.

At the college Sidney tells her fears and ideas to another survivor of the previous massacre, Randy Meeks, but he refuses to accept them. They are joined by Sidney's new boyfriend, Derek. Chief Hartley, in charge of the investigation, gives a press conference and says that there's no evidence that a serial killer is involved. Then

Sidney encounters another survivor from Woodsboro, Dewey Riley, a former police deputy. He has come to the college to make sure that she is safe.

Sidney is then confronted by Gale Weathers and Cotton Weary, the man who Sidney had accused of murdering her mother. Furious at Gale for putting her on the spot yet again, she punches her (yet again). Soon afterwards Gale runs into Dewey, who is also annoyed with her for making him look like a dumb country hayseed in her book (not too difficult).

That night Sidney and her room-mate Hallie attend a sorority party. At another sorority house nearby, student 'CiCi' Cooper watches TV. She believes she is alone in the building. Then she gets a phone call from a man who asks her 'Do you want to die tonight?' Another member of the sorority appears, but she is on her way out. Alone again, CiCi is attacked by a masked figure, Ghostface. Trapped on an upstairs balcony, she is stabbed and then thrown to her death.

The party breaks up when news is received that something has happened at the other sorority house. While Derek waits outside, Sidney goes back into the building, now apparently empty, to fetch her jacket. But the killer, Ghostface, suddenly appears, armed with a knife, and attempts to kill her. She manages to escape outside and Derek enters to search for her assailant. Dewey arrives and finds Derek with his arm gashed. Derek claims that the killer did it but Dewey is suspicious.

The following day Gale learns from Chief Hartley that the killer is trying to follow in the footsteps of the Woodsboro killer, Billy Loomis, as the new victims share the same names as Billy's victims. Hartley assigns two detectives to act as Sidney's bodyguards, much to Derek's annoyance. Sidney's doubts about Derek are growing.

In the college cafeteria Derek attempts to win back her affections by serenading her in front of everyone (his choice of song, unfortunately, is 'I Think I Love You' from *Top Gun*). The ploy appears to have worked on Sidney because she accepts his fraternity letters as a token of his love. Later, when taking part in a rehearsal of a Greek play in the college theatre, Sidney, who is playing Cassandra, believes she spots Ghostface among the masked chorus. She cracks up.

The next day, Gale is discussing the situation with Randy and Dewey on the campus lawn when Randy gets a call from the killer on his mobile. While Gale and Dewey go off to hunt for a likely suspect, Randy is dragged into Gale's outside broadcast van and stabbed to death.

In the college library Sidney gets a message on her computer screen: 'You are going to die'. While her police escorts search for the culprit, Sidney is accosted by Cotton Weary, who wants her to join him on the Diane Sawyer TV show for a large sum of money. When she refuses, he threatens her... and is arrested by her police protectors. Chief Hartley, however, has no choice but to release him. The Police Chief then arranges for Sidney to be moved to a safe place...

Meanwhile, Gale and Dewey, their mutual antipathy now turned into mutual affection, have joined forces. Gale thinks the killer may have been caught on videotape by her cameraman, Joel. They enter the college's auditorium to find a VCR. While Joel's footage is being screened on a monitor, Gale and Dewey start getting passionate... but then Gale spots that the footage now being screened is not Joel's. Instead there are shots on the screen of the murder victims, and then a shot of Gale and Dewey in the auditorium. Then they see the Ghostface peering down at them from the control room. Dewey races (well, *limps*) upstairs to the control room, and finds it empty. But then Gale is attacked by Ghostface and flees into the corridor.

Hiding in a TV studio, Gale sees Ghostface enter the adjacent control room. Ghostface vanishes, but then Dewey enters the control room. Gale tries to warn him but can't make herself heard through the thick soundproof window. Then, to her horror, she sees Ghostface stab Dewey...

An aggrieved Derek watches Sidney being driven away, with Hallie, by her two police guards. Then Derek is grabbed by his fraternity members, who are determined to punish him for giving Sidney his fraternity letters. He is taken to the college auditorium, partly stripped and tied to a suspended prop from the Greek play.

The police car stops at some temporary traffic lights... and then the Ghostface strikes. One of the police guards is killed instantly. The other one gets out of the car and is also attacked. Then Ghostface

CASEY BECKER HAD THE MISFORTUNE TO BE THE FIRST TO EVER HEAR THOSE DREADED WORDS OVER THE PHONE, "DO YOU LIKE SCARY MOVIES?" THE NEXT THING SHE KNEW, SHE WAS IN ONE.

TATUM RILEY MADE THE MISTAKE OF LEAVING THE PARTY TO VISIT THE BASEMENT. WHAT HAPPENED TO HER DOWN THERE SHOULDN'T HAVE HAPPENED TO A DOG.

STUART MACHER THOUGHT THAT HE AND BEST BUDDY BILLY LOOMIS COULD GET AWAY WITH MURDER BUT SIDNEY PRESCOTT TAUGHT HIM THAT WATCHING TOO MUCH TV COULD BE FATAL.

BILLY LOOMIS SET THE WHOLE SERIES OF 'GHOSTFACE' MURDERS IN MOTION BUT THANKS TO HIS EX-GIRLFRIEND, SIDNEY, HE DIDN'T SURVIVE TO SEE THE SEQUEL.

MAUREEN EVANS LEARNT THAT THERE'S A FATAL DOWNSIDE TO ATTENDING THE PREMIERE OF A SCARY MOVIE – ESPECIALLY IF IT'S CALLED 'STAB'.

CASEY COOPER DISCOVERED TO HER COST THAT THERE'S NEVER A VAMPIRE SLAYER AROUND WHEN YOU REALLY NEED ONE.

RANDY MEEKS THOUGHT HE KNEW ALL THE RULES NEEDED TO SURVIVE A HORROR MOVIE, BUT THAT STILL DIDN'T STOP HIM FROM BECOMING A BLOODY CADAVER.

MRS LOOMIS, OUT TO AVENGE THE DEATH OF HER SON, BILLY, CAME TO A STICKY END WHEN SHE TANGLED WITH HIS EX-GIRLFRIEND, WHO HAS A KNACK FOR DISPATCHING MEMBERS OF THE LOOMIS FAMILY.

COTTON WEARY, FALSELY ACCUSED OF THE MURDER OF SIDNEY'S MOTHER, JUSTIFIABLY FELT HARD DONE BY...BUT THAT LED HIM INTO A SERIOUS SITUATION.

JOHN MILTON IS A FILM PRODUCER WITH A SHADY PAST AND THIS PAST PROVES FATAL WHEN HE DECIDES TO PRODUCE A MOVIE CALLED 'STAB 3'.

DETECTIVE KINCAID HAS THE UNENVIABLE TASK OF TRYING TO KEEP THE CAST OF 'STAB 3' ALIVE - BUT THERE IS A CONSOLATION PRIZE IN THE FORM OF SIDNEY PRESCOTT.

ACTRESS JENNIFER JOLIE THINKS THE ROLE OF PLAYING GALE WEATHERS IN 'STAB 3' IS A GREAT CAREER MOVE, UNTIL IT LEADS HER TO AN EARLY GRAVE.

SARAH DARLING IS HORRIFIED WHEN THE CAST OF HER NEW FILM ARE BEING KILLED OFF ONE BY ONE - ESPECIALLY AS SHE'S HIGH ON THE VICTIM LIST - AND WANTS TO CHANGE HER AGENT BUT IT'S TOO LATE.

ACTRESS ANGELINA TYLER, WHO IS PLAYING SIDNEY PRESCOTT IN "STAB 3", APPEARS TO BE A PICTURE OF INNOCENT SWEETNESS, BUT A MURKY PAST LEADS TO A FATAL ENCOUNTER WITH GHOSTFACE.

GALE WEATHERS GOT A BOOK AND THREE MOVIES OUT OF THE WOODSBORO MURDERS BUT AT THE END OF IT ALL WAS LEFT FEELING THAT BEING AN INVESTIGATIVE JOURNALIST WASN'T ALL IT WAS CUT OUT TO BE.

DWIGHT "DEWEY" RILEY'S INVOLVEMENT WITH SIDNEY PRESCOTT AND HER PROBLEMS COST HIM HIS SISTER, HIS JOB AND LEFT HIM WITH A PERMANENT LIMP, BUT HE KEPT COMING BACK FOR MORE.

SIDNEY PRESCOTT WOULD BE JUSTIFIED IN FEELING THAT SHE'S JINXED, PARTICULARLY AS ANYONE CLOSE TO HER HAS A TENDENCY TO END UP EXTREMELY DEAD.

KEVIN WILLIAMSON STRUCK GOLD WHEN HE CAME UP WITH THE IDEA FOR A FILM CALLED 'SCARY MOVIE'. IT BECAME 'SCREAM' AND MADE MOVIE HISTORY.

WES CRAVEN TOPPED A SUCCESSFUL, AND CONTROVERSIAL, CAREER IN HORROR MOVIES WHEN HE AGREED TO DIRECT 'SCREAM' AND ITS SEQUELS, WHICH LED TO MORE SUCCESS... AND MUCH MORE CONTROVERSY.

gets into the driver's seat... and Sidney and Hallie are trapped in the back because the police car has no interior door handles.

Then the second police guard leaps onto the car's bonnet. Ghostface drives off and crashes the car, killing the guard. Ghostface appears to have been knocked unconscious. Sidney and Hallie are forced to climb over him to get out of the car. They are about to run to safety when Sidney, unwisely in the circumstances, decides she must return to the car and unmask Ghostface. But she finds the car empty... and then Ghostface suddenly attacks Hallie and kills her. Sidney flees.

Sidney ends up in the now empty auditorium. Derek, unconscious now and still tied to the stage prop, is lowered from the flies. Ghostface appears and removes his mask, revealing himself to be Mickey. He tells Sidney that he and Derek are working together. Sidney believes him... until Mickey shoots Derek dead.

Then Debbie Salt makes an appearance with Gale as her prisoner. Debbie turns out to be the mother of the original killer, Billy Loomis, whom Sidney had shot dead in Woodsboro. Mrs Loomis wants revenge, but first shoots Mickey, as she is no longer in need of his assistance. As he falls, he shoots Gale, who falls into the orchestra pit.

Mrs Loomis is about to kill Sidney when Cotton Weary, also armed, appears. She tries to persuade him to join forces with her but, after some hesitation, Cotton shoots her. Then Gale emerges from the pit, wounded but not seriously so. When Mickey makes the inevitable surprise return to life, both Gale and Sidney shoot him... and then Sidney puts a bullet through Mrs Loomis's forehead to make sure she isn't about to spring any surprises of her own.

The film ends with Gale overjoyed to see that Dewey has once again miraculously survived, while a gloomy Sidney walks away from the scene, once again having lost a boyfriend, a best friend (plus a second best friend this time) and numerous acquaintances.

CREDITS

Director . . . . Wes Craven

Screenplay . . . . Kevin Williamson

Cinematographer . . . . Peter Deming

Production Designer . . . . Bob Ziembicki

Original Music . . . . Marco Beltrami, Danny Elfman

Producers . . . . Cathy Konrad, Marianne Maddalena

Co-Producer . . . . Daniel Lupi

Executive Producers . . . . Bob Weinstein
Harvey Weinstein
Kevin Williamson

CAST

Dwight 'Dewey' Riley	David Arquette
Sidney	Neve Campbell
Gale Weathers	Courteney Cox
Casey 'CiCi' Cooper	Sarah Michelle Gellar
Randy Meeks	Jamie Kennedy
Joel, the Cameraman	Duane Martin
Debbie Salt	Laurie Metcalf
Hallie	Elise Neal
Derek	Jerry O'Connell
Mickey	Timothy Olyphant
Maureen Evans	Jada Pinkett
Cotton Weary	Liev Schreiber
Chief Lewis Hartley	Lewis Arquette
Sister Lois	Rebecca Gayheart
Sister Murphy	Portia de Rossi
Phil Stevens	Omar Epps
Sidney in *Stab*	Tori Spelling
Casey in *Stab*	Heather Graham
Cotton's Interviewer	Kevin Williamson

SCR3AM

SCREAM 3
THE MOVIE

At the start of *Scream 3* we see Cotton Weary (Liev Schreiber) stuck in a traffic jam near the Hollywood Bowl and talking loudly on his cellphone. We later learn that he now has his own nationally syndicated TV chat show, *100% Cotton*, and he's due to film a scene in *Stab 3*, but as he complains to someone over the phone, he doesn't really want to do a cameo in 'a cheap slasher flick'. The irony here is that Liev Schreiber could be accused of doing exactly that – a cameo in a cheap slasher flick. The third and final *Scream* film makes the most of its status as part of a trilogy. This is highlighted by the video tape recorded by the late Randy Meeks (Jamie Kennedy) on which he explains 'the rules of trilogies', referring to *The Godfather Part III* and *Return of the Jedi*. While it's good to see the much-missed Randy again, his theories about trilogies are a little difficult to swallow. Neither the *Godfather* or the *Star Wars* films were originally planned as trilogies, they just turned out that way – as did the *Scream* series. In fact, about the only valid rule you could have about film trilogies is that nobody deliberately sets out to make one (it's only in retrospect that film makers start stating such claims). But, the big question on fans lips was whether *Scream 3* is as satisfying as the first two – and the answer to that is, yes – in parts.

New scriptwriter Ehren Kruger, brought in as Kevin Williamson wasn't available, does an adequate job as his substitute but his weaknesses in certain areas make you realize that Williamson was cleverer than one gave him credit for. For example, none of the new characters is as well-developed as any of the characters introduced in the first two movies. Also some of the plotting seems overly awkward and convoluted, but then Kruger was faced with the almost impossible task of introducing a new killer who was somehow connected with what happened in the first film. Kruger's one original gimmick, the electronic voice-imitating device, is used repeatedly but not in very imaginative ways. However, he does have a deft hand with dialogue and some of the best scenes revolve around the film studio where *Stab 3* is being shot (the studio scenes were apparently shot at Paramount).

One of the highlights of the film is the double-act between Courteney Cox Arquette and Parker Posey. Posey, previously best known for her roles in independent movies, is playing an actress, Jennifer Jolie who is playing Gale Weathers in *Stab 3*, and by a stroke of luck, the two do look very similar (though Cox Arquette is sporting a new hairstyle). A classic exchange between the pair is when Gale accuses Jennifer of being '...a straight-to-video version of me', while Jennifer complains, 'Like I'm going to win an award playing *you*.' And when it turns out that the killer is murdering the actors in *Stab 3* in the same order that their characters die in the script Jennifer is alarmed to discover she's next in line. So she says to Gale, 'Everywhere you go, I'm going to follow you, so if he wants to kill you, you'll be there to be killed, and he won't need to kill me.' To be honest, Posey's performance, basically a clever parody of Cox Arquette playing Gale Weathers, is better than the real thing, but then Posey acts rings around everyone else in the movie – without even seeming to try.

The killing-in-sequence gimmick sets up a wry reference to real-life events surrounding the making of *Scream 3*. When Detective Mark Kincaid (Patrick Dempsey) says that it should be simple to predict the third victim, the producer, John Milton (Lance Henriksen) disagrees, pointing out, 'There were three different versions of the script to keep the ending off the Internet. I don't know which one the killer read.' Then comes another joke involving a fax machine when the killer faxes them revised pages of the screenplay which he's written himself...

Among the newcomers to the cast is Emily Mortimer who plays a seemingly angelic young actress by the appropriate name of Angelina Tyler who is playing the role of Sidney in *Stab 3*. When the murders begin her line: 'I'm starting to see why Tori Spelling and David Schwimmer didn't want to come back...' continues the self-referential *Scream* tradition. Another newcomer is Jenny McCarthy as Sarah Darling, a bimbo-style actress hired to play an anonymous victim in *Stab 3*. After complaining about being 35 and yet still being required to play 21-year-olds, she gets one of the film's biggest laughs when she refuses to do a scene in a shower because she's seen Hitchcock's *Vertigo*. 'Jesus, I gotta get a new agent!' she exclaims when she realizes what she's landed herself in. But it's too late – like her character in *Stab 3*, she ends up on the wrong end of a knife. Among a number of amusing cameos in *Scream 3*, Carrie Fisher's stands out in particular. She plays a disgruntled studio archivist who was a former actress who gets to complain, 'I was up for Princess Leia, but you know who gets it... the one who sleeps with George Lucas.' And Patrick Warburton makes an impression in his small part as a celebrity security guard, Steven Stone, whose past clients, he claims, have included, Salman Rushdie and Julia Roberts.

One of the disappointments in *Scream 3* concerns its nominal star, Neve Campbell. She hardly features at in the first half of the movie and when her character, Sidney, finally does arrive in Hollywood where the murders are taking place, the script keeps misplacing her. It's as if writer Ehren Kruger couldn't find anything worthwhile for her to do this time round. However, as Craven has pointed out, the real protagonists of *Scream 3* are Dewey (David Arquette plays him with a limp although the paralysed arm he had in *Scream 2* seems to have been miraculously cured), Gale Weathers and to a lesser extent, Jennifer Jolie (with hindsight, Parker Posey should have been given a much bigger part). On the rare occasions that Campbell is centre stage, she appears to be in a different movie to everyone else. You get the feeling that she only agreed to do the third film provided the script gave her the opportunity to do some 'serious' acting.

Scream 3 works better as a satire on the film industry than as a horror movie. Overall it's much lighter in tone (Campbell's performance excepted) than the previous two and while the body count is very high the murders themselves are much less graphic and bloody than before. None of the death scenes has the impact of that of Casey (Drew Barrymore) in *Scream* or of Maureen (Jada Pinkett) in *Scream 2*. While there are plenty of scary moments and shocks there is nothing to equal the tension in, say, the sequence in *Scream 2* where Sidney and Hallie have to crawl over the unconscious Ghostface in order to get out of the crashed car. The frenetic climax in John Milton's Hollywood mansion, which is full of secret panels, trapdoors, secret rooms and horror props, is more reminiscent of a much earlier style of horror movie (*The Cat and the Canary* or, if one wanted to be really unkind, *Abbot and Costello Meet the Wolfman...*). But for all that, it *is* good fun.

The only really serious flaw in the movie is the identity of the killer. It comes as no real surprise when it's revealed that Roman Bridger (Scott Foley), the director of *Stab 3*, is Ghostface, even though he'd earlier faked his death, because by the time of the unmasking, alternative suspects have become thin on the ground. Despite Kruger's elaborate rationale to justify Bridger's links with the earlier murders (it turns out that he was the illegitimate son of Sidney's mother, Maurine, and therefore Sidney's half-brother and so on) it's not the slightest bit convincing. In the end it doesn't really matter *who* the killer is, which is ironic when you consider the extreme lengths that Miramax went to keep the ending a secret, as that's not what *Scream 3* is all about (unlike, for example, *The Sixth Sense*, where the surprise ending is relevant to what's gone on before). As long as fans don't go to see *Scream 3* in order to leave the cinema muttering, 'Well, who'd have expected *that!*' and go to see it to have fun, then *Scream 3* delivers the goods.

Scream 3 opened in America on 4 February 2000 and enjoyed a box office return over the weekend of $35.2 million, setting a record for Miramax. During its first three days the film also earned more than the combined total of every other film in the top ten. 'This is beyond our expectations for sure,' said Miramax boss, Bob

Weinstein, in something of an understatement. Critical reaction was mixed but generally favourable – the most common criticism levelled at the movie concerned the identity of the killer and the lack of substance in the characters. As Roger Ebert wrote in the *Chicago Sun-Times*, 'Anyone who would reveal the identity of the killer in *Scream 3* would in any event be the lowest form of life, since the secret is absolutely unguessable. Why? Because the identity is absolutely arbitrary. It could be anyone in the movie or (this would be a neat twist) none of the above. The characters are so thin they're transparent. They function primarily to scream, split up when they should stick together, go alone into basements and dark rooms, and make ironic references to horror clichés and earlier movies in the series. Director Wes Craven covered the self-aware horror genre splendidly in *Wes Craven's New Nightmare* and this is the lite version.' But *Variety* probably best sums up the movie as a whole: '*Scream 3* is a crafty and well-crafted wrap-up that really does bring a satisfying sense of closure to the franchise.'

SCREAM 3
BEHIND
THE SCENES

The gestation of *Scream 3* came complete with a set of dire rumours that suggested the project was in deep trouble from the start. Rumour one was that Neve Campbell wouldn't be returning for a third outing as *Scream* Queen Sidney Prescott. It was said that she was annoyed with Miramax because they wouldn't let her star in their production of John Dahl's *Rounders* (in the event, she was lucky she didn't appear in that movie). Rumour two claimed that Wes Craven was showing solidarity with Campbell and refusing to direct *Scream 3* because of Campbell's absence. Then came rumour number three, that had Heather Graham being offered the Campbell role but turning it down because of other commitments, leaving the producers desperately searching for a replacement. Rumour four had it that the now husband and wife team of Courteney Cox and David Arquette had jumped the *Scream* ship as well. And rumour five was that Kevin Williamson wouldn't be writing the screenplay of *Scream 3* because he too had other commitments.

Of all the rumours concerning the movie, only the last one turned out to be true. Williamson did write a treatment for the film but didn't have time to write the screenplay. In the event even Williamson's treatment wasn't used and he was replaced by writer Ehren Kruger (*Arlington Road*) who came up with a new story and consequently, wrote the screenplay. Neve Campbell, however, did return for *Scream 3*, as did the Arquettes and Wes Craven. According to Craven, the rumours about the three stars being reluctant to reprise their roles, and his own threatened bail-out, were just that – groundless rumours. 'It wasn't really that difficult getting the core group of actors back,' he told *Fangoria* and *Cinefantastique* magazines while still shooting the film. 'If anything was difficult, it was the scheduling. We were dealing with a group of actors who are very busy. But there was a willingness on the part of everyone to do the third film. Nobody believes us but there is not going to be another *Scream* after this, and so there was the added incentive on everybody's part to finish what they'd started. But it's very difficult because both Neve and Courteney are back in their TV series, so we're shooting in the so-called leisure time from their TV shows. We've been working on weekends and so forth, but it's not that different from the way the other two *Scream* movies were made. They've always been worked around Courteney and Neve's schedules.' To ensure that Neve Campbell returned for the third film Miramax resorted to a tactic they'd used with other artists, including Craven himself – they offered her backing on a couple of film projects of her own. But also, according to Campbell, 'I just felt that I owed it to the fans of the first two.'

As for the rumours concerning Wes Craven's own involvement, he said, 'I was pretty much always committed to doing all three films. I always saw it, almost from the onset, as a trilogy. I always like the fact that rather than concentrating on a franchise killer who keeps coming back, like Freddy or Jason, we were focusing on the development of the characters...with a trilogy, you keep the same central core of positive characters, and then you can have a generational thing like in *The Godfather*.'

There were also many rumours circulating about the nature of the plot of *Scream 3*. One of the most persistent had Sidney, having been a drama student in the second film, now in Hollywood and acting in a horror exploitation film. When Kevin Williamson was asked about this possible scenario, he playfully told *Fade In* magazine in mid-1999, 'Well, that's the obvious route to take, because in

Scream 2 Sidney was a theatre major... we're probably going to go down a bunch of different paths. There were so many ideas. Interestingly enough, we've leaked some false information.' Which suggests that Williamson himself was probably leaking even more false information at the time. 'The big surprise, of course, is who's the killer. That's what's so great about *Scream 3* – the ending. There are so many fun things in the movie, like where they're just chatting and they're saying, "You know what? It's so over. Why are we even making this movie? The horror genre's over." And they're like, "We're different. We started it. We can end it." ' Williamson gave the impression that he was more than happy to see the film marking the end of the teenage horror genre, and compared himself to the Gale Weathers character in *Scream 3*, 'She makes comments like, "Oh, come on. Just make up some story, cast a bunch of WB actresses so we can kill them and we'll be fine." '

But, as mentioned earlier, Williamson had nothing to do with either the story or the script of *Scream 3*. He dearly wanted to write the third film but was then involved with both the post-production of his movie *Killing Mrs Tingle* and the shooting of his new TV series *Wasteland* and suggested to Bob Weinstein at Miramax that they delay *Scream 3* until the following year. Interestingly he cited the fresh controversy over movie violence as a good reason for postponing the movie. But Miramax were committed to making the film in mid-1999 when both Neve Campbell and Courteney Cox had a window in their punishing TV schedules. Williamson did write an outline for the movie but it was again set in Woodsboro with the plot revolving around high school students – both the producers and Craven thought it would be best to move the story forward rather than return to familiar territory.

A substitute writer had to be found quickly. Bob Weinstein suggested to Craven that they use a scriptwriter who Weinstein had worked with previously – a young man by the name of Ehren Kruger. 'I thought at first it was a joke,' said Craven, automatically presuming he was some relation of Freddie Krueger. Ehren Kruger had worked with Weinstein on John Frankenheimer's *Reindeer Games*, but had gained the most plaudits for writing the thriller *Arlington*

Road starring Jeff Bridges and Tim Robbins. Craven was initially dubious that Kruger could come up with an entirely new approach to *Scream 3* in the limited time available. 'Quite frankly, I thought Bob was crazy, because it was going to be a complete page one re-thinking of everything – nothing was going to be used from Kevin's original treatment.' But in just four days Kruger came through with the goods, impressing everyone concerned, and was given the go-ahead to write the screenplay. Again, it was a task he had to complete in a relatively short amount of time, and again he impressed everyone with the result. Craven said, 'He's an extraordinary workman. He went in trying to write in the style of the previous two films – he knew them very well – and yet he was able to contribute a wicked sense of humour that was all his own. He turned in a fantastic first draft. We were very happy with what we got from him. He's really like the next Kevin Williamson. There were plenty of changes later, but that's just part of the process. *Scream 3* hasn't been a patched-together thing.' Craven went on to explain that the final version of the screenplay was the result of a great deal of collaboration, not only between himself and Kruger, and producers Marianne Maddalena and Cathy Konrad, but also with Neve Campbell, Courteney Cox and David Arquette. Of the plot itself Craven said, 'Sidney has not gone to Hollywood to become an actress in a B-horror movie. But there is a picture being made as part of our story, which is one of the sequels in the *Stab* series, the movie within the movie. Sidney does get involved in it, but not as an actress.

The movie within the movie is *Stab 3* and results in some mind-bending shifts in character identification. For example, Parker Posey is Jennifer Jolie, an actor playing Courteney Cox's character, Gale Weathers in *Stab 3*. *Stab 3*'s director Roman Bridger is played by Scott Foley and the producer, John Milton, by Lance Henriksen (any similarity between these two characters and Wes Craven and Bob Weinstein is surely coincidental). There are also cameos from veteran horror film-maker Roger Corman and Kevin *Clerks*, *Dogma* Smith.

Stab 3 is a film version of the events in *Scream 2* and when it goes into production Sidney once again finds herself the target of a mystery killer. She goes to Hollywood to try and uncover the connection between the two, and no sooner does she arrive at the set than the director of *Stab 3* (Scott Foley) is murdered, along with one of the actresses. Gale Weathers, who now has her own TV talk show, and her boyfriend, Dwight 'Dewey' Riley, are once again drawn into the investigation. Both of the latter characters have more prominent roles in *Scream 3* and they become the main investigators of the series of murders. According to Craven, 'Courteney and David are certainly the lead couple in the movie...they have a tremendous number of scenes together and they are kind of the narrators of the story.' Even so Craven insists that Neve Campbell's character, Sidney, remains the central one. 'The story all revolves around Sidney and revelations about her past. It's a summation and final revelation of her life and history, so Neve is still very much the star.'

As with Craven's *New Nightmare* which also revolved around a film within a film, *Scream 3* provides the director with the opportunity to make some pertinent comments about Hollywood and the nature of film-making in general. Craven and his unit filmed all over Hollywood and Los Angeles, utilising familiar settings such as Hollywood Boulevard and the famous Hollywood sign on the hillside overlooking Hollywood. 'I think everyone who contributed to the script put in some inside jokes about studio executives and that sort of thing,' said Craven, 'but I believe we've also been harder on ourselves than somebody from the outside might have been.' The crew kept telling Craven that he should appear in a cameo scene but Craven resisted the temptation. 'We haven't gone as far as *A New Nightmare* where I played myself...Directing this was a big enough part, believe me.'

With the making of the film within the film, *Stab 3*, Craven and his team were able to establish visual reference points to the first two *Scream* movies. 'It's also fun to go in and out of sets that are identical to places you've seen in *Scream*', said Craven, 'and then suddenly find yourself off the sets and on a soundstage. It's the jarring realization that not everything that appears to be real, is really real. Even though Sidney is not part of the actual production of *Stab 3* she gets drawn into its world and is exposed to the false image it expresses of her own life and tragedies. She finds herself walking onto the set and seeing, for example, her own home, but it's not really like her house, of course – it's what the film makers *think* it should be like. There's a lot of that kind of thing, the examination of reality versus the illusion presented by films. That's one of the fun themes of *Scream 3*.'

And is *Scream 3* really the last *Scream* in the series? 'I certainly won't do another one,' declared Craven, 'nor will Neve or any of the rest of the original team. We're all moving on...' Despite this, Miramax boss Bob Weinstein has hinted that if *Scream 3* makes as much money as the previous two films then the company might make another *Scream* in about four years' time, but it would be a totally different story with a different cast of characters.

Who knows? The year 2004 might just see the release of *Scream 4*.

EHREN KRUGER

The 27-year-old Ehren Kruger, already hailed by Wes Craven as 'the new Kevin Williamson', has made a sizeable splash in Hollywood within a remarkably short space of time. Born in the state of New York in 1972, he attended New York University's film school where he studied screenwriting. His first script to reach the production stage was for the TV movie *Killers in the House* in 1997. Directed by Michael Schultz, it was an off-the-wall thriller about four bank robbers who take over a house while on the run from the police, and starred Mario Van Peebles. It attracted enough attention within the industry for Kruger to be offered feature film writing assignments and he hasn't stopped working since.

His follow-up screenplay was for the superior paranoid thriller *Arlington Road* (1998), directed by Mark Pellington and starring Jeff Bridges and Tim Robbins. Less successful was the high-tech thriller *New World Disorder*, directed by Richard Spence and featuring Hari Dhillon, Tara Fitzgerald and Rutger Hauer, but by then he'd come to the attention of Bob Weinstein at Miramax. Weinstein quickly signed him up and had him working on two assignments for the company in 1999. One was *Impostor*, based on a Philip K. Dick science fiction story, starring Gary Sinese and Madeline Stowe and directed by Gary Fleder. The other was *Reindeer Games* (also known as *Deception*), a John Frankenheimer-directed thriller starring Ben Affleck as a recently released convict reluctantly caught up in a plan to rob a casino. So satisfied was Weinstein with Kruger's work on these two films that when Kevin Williamson initiated a crisis by announcing that he didn't have time to write the third *Scream* film, Weinstein immediately thought of Kruger...

So it was that Kruger received the fateful phone call from Bob Weinstein asking him if he would consider filling in for the absent Williamson. He was a fan of the first two films, and keen to work with Wes Craven, so he readily agreed. After watching the earlier films again, and reading Williamson's treatment, he wrote his own treatment for *Scream 3* but, as he told *Fangoria* magazine, he didn't get it quite right. 'I had the Sidney character written too much like Linda Hamilton in *Terminator 2*. Wes Craven had to say to me, "It's good... but that's not really the character here." He had to steer me back.' Understandably, Kruger found it difficult because he hadn't lived with the characters in the same way that Craven and the actors had, and he admitted that they knew the characters much better than he did. 'So a lot of it was learning and listening to Wes and the actors.'

Another problem facing Kruger was that everyone was worried about the story's violence in the wake of the Columbine High School massacre and the anti-Hollywood backlash that had generated in the media. The decision on what direction to take with the script varied from day to day, and at one point Miramax even seriously considered making *Scream 3* a violence-free zone with a total absence of blood. But, according to Kruger, Craven put his foot down and said, 'Be serious, guys. Either we make a *Scream* movie or we make a movie and call it something else. But if it's a *Scream* movie it has to have certain standards.' Kruger agreed with Craven's approach: 'It needs to be, at points, scary.' Even so, he feels that *Scream 3* is not as graphic or as dark as the first two films.

> *I feel it does emphasize the comedy and the satire a little more, at least in the first half of the movie. It also delves a little more into the mythology of these characters...These movies are basically whodunnits. They're Scooby Doo and Nancy Drew... they're mysteries with room to laugh and to*

be frightened, but what the plots really lead to is the question – 'Who is the person, or persons, behind the curtain?'

Future Kruger assignments include a remake of the 1958 *Bell, Book and Candle*, a romantic comedy which originally starred James Stewart as the publisher who falls in love with a beautiful witch played by Kim Novak; and *Mythic*, a horror film about a fire investigator who discovers a demonic cause behind a series of mysterious fires. But, for the moment, Ehren Kruger finds himself an integral part of the *Scream* phenomenon, while admitting he doesn't know yet if *Scream 3* will mark the end of that particular horror genre – at least for a time. 'If it is the last word on the "smart slasher movie", it's defiantly sending it into hiatus on a high note.'

STAR FILES

DAVID ARQUETTE

David Arquette's character, Dwight 'Dewey' Riley, has appeared in all three *Scream* movies, a record only matched by his co-stars, Neve Campbell, Courteney Cox and Liev Schreiber. Arquette comes from an acting family. His siblings, Rosanna, Patricia, Alexis and Richmond, are all in the business, as is his father, Lewis Arquette (who played the police chief in *Scream 2* but is best known for his role in *The Waltons*). His grandfather, Cliff Arquette, was a comedy actor on radio and TV, who usually played a hillbilly character called Charlie Weaver. Born in Virginia in 1971, David Arquette has been acting since the age of 15 and much of his early career was on TV. His pre-*Scream* film appearances included roles in *Buffy the Vampire Slayer* (1992), *Airheads* (1994), *Beautiful Girls* (1996) and *Johns* (1996), in which he made a strong impression as a drugged-up street hustler. After *Scream 2* he appeared in *Ravenous* (1999) and co-starred with Drew Barrymore in *Never Been Kissed* (1999). He's been a friend of Barrymore since his early years as a teenage actor. 'It's crazy growing up in Hollywood, which is why there is such a close bond between us.'

Interviewed shortly after making the first *Scream* movie, Arquette said of playing Dewey, 'I love the comedy side of the character – comedy is about who we are. Wes is supercool and wisecracking. He flashed on set and dressed up in Courteney Cox's outfit,' thus revealing a side to Wes Craven hitherto concealed. And of the future Mrs Arquette, Courteney Cox, he said at the time, 'No one quite realizes what a deep actress she is.' The admiration was clearly mutual: shortly after making *Scream*, he guest-starred in an episode of *Friends*. The now husband-and-wife team have recently starred in *The Shrink Is In* (1999), which they also co-produced.

LANCE HENRIKSEN

Riddled with bullets from Big Arnie in *The Terminator*, sliced in half by the Mother Alien in *Aliens*, and sizzled by the sun in the vampire movie *Near Dark*, Lance Henriksen has had a hard time of it in the previous genre films in which he's appeared. So the prognosis for his character in *Scream 3* – John Milton, the producer of the ill-fated movie, *Stab 3* – is not good. With a name like John Milton, you're asking for trouble.

Actually this is not the first Wes Craven production that the 59-year-old actor has been involved in – he appeared in the 1995 HBO science fiction/horror movie *Mind Ripper*, which was filmed in Bulgaria by Craven's son Jonathan. In that film Henriksen was the creator of a lethal cyborg that runs around eating people's brains.

The craggy-faced character actor has had few starring roles in feature movies, one exception being in the underrated *Pumpkinhead* (1988), directed by effects wizard Stan Winston. But on TV, apart from playing Charles Bronson in *Reason for Living: The Jill Ireland Story*, he starred in his own series, *Millennium*, the grim spin-off from *The X-Files*, in which he played the less-than-jolly Frank Black, who has a psychic affinity with serial killers.

A graduate of the Actors Studio, Henriksen has been appearing in films since 1972, and while his first big role was in *Dog Day Afternoon*, casting directors of genre films seem to have kept him at the top of their lists in the years since then. Apart from the ones made by his good friend James Cameron (starting with *Piranha II: The Spawning* in 1981), he has featured in other such genre movies as *Mansion of the Doomed, Damien: Omen Two, The Horror Show, The Pit and the Pendulum* and now *Scream 3*. Maybe there's something about his face…

JENNY McCARTHY

Jenny McCarthy, who plays Sarah Darling in *Scream 3* (Darling is the actress who plays Tatum Riley in *Stab 3*, the character originally played by Rose McGowan in *Scream*), has mainly made a career out of playing herself in films and on TV and videos.

Born in Illinois in 1972, McCarthy had planned to become a nurse but dropped out of nursing school when she decided to become a model instead. It was a struggle for a time until she was chosen as *Playboy* Playmate of the Month for October 1993 and everything changed. She's since played herself in such productions as *The Best of Jenny McCarthy* (a *Playboy* video), *Jenny McCarthy – The Playboy Years* (another *Playboy* video), *The Jenny McCarthy Show* (a 1997 TV series), *Jenny* (another TV series) and *Playboy Playmates of the Year: The '90s* (another *Playboy* video). Apart from her role in *Scream 3*, one of her rare film appearances where she didn't play herself was in *Things to Do in Denver When You're Dead*. In that she played... a nurse.

PARKER POSEY

Parker Posey, the 'Queen of the Indies', in a *Scream* movie? Yes, she's just one of the surprises in *Scream 3* and another indicator of just how fashionable it's become for actors to accept a role in the *Scream* series.

Born in Baltimore in November 1968, she moved to Laurel, Mississippi at the age of 11 and then attended the North Carolina School for the Arts (funny how North Carolina figures somewhere in the background of so many of the people in this book). She moved to New York and majored in acting at the SUNY Purchase College, and while still a student got her first professional acting job in the TV soap opera *As the World Turns* in 1991.

It was her role in the TV mini-series *Armistead Maupin's Tales of the City* (1993) that brought her to the attention of independent film-makers like Hal Hartley, who cast her in three of his movies, *Amateur* (1994), *Flirt* (1995) and *Henry Fool* (1997). Her first starring role was in another independent production, Daisy von Scherler

Mayer's *Party Girl* in 1995 (which also featured fellow *Scream 3* actor Liev Schreiber), and she had leading roles in two other much acclaimed indie productions, *The Doom Generation* (1995) and *The Daytrippers* (1996).

A friend of Nora Ephron, Posey has had parts in three of her films, *Sleepless in Seattle* (1993 – though her scenes were deleted in the cutting room), *Mixed Nuts* (1994) and *You've Got Mail* (1998). And now, in *Scream 3*, confusingly she plays an actress, Jennifer Jolie, playing Courteney Cox's *alter ego*, Gale Weathers in the movie-within-the-movie, *Stab 3*.

PATRICK DEMPSEY

Patrick Dempsey, who has the singular honour of portraying David Arquette in *Scream 3* (he plays Detective Mark Kincaid) has been appearing on TV and in films since 1985, but his filmography features a lot of lesser-known titles.

Born in Maine in 1966, his original ambition was to be a circus clown and when he was a teenager he was placed third in his age group at the National Jugglers Convention. His first film role was in *Heaven Help Us* (a.k.a. *Catholic Boys*) in 1985. Since then he's had roles in such films as *Meatballs III*, *In the Mood* (or *The Woo Woo Kid*), *Loverboy*, *Happy Together*, *Bank Robber*, *Ava's Magical Adventure*, *The Escape*, *Hugo Pool*, *Outbreak*, *Denial* and *There's No Fish Food in Heaven*. His TV appearances have included the mini-series *JFK: Reckless Youth* (in which he played the young John F. Kennedy), *Twenty Thousand Leagues under the Sea* and *Dostoevsky's Crime and Punishment*.

EMILY MORTIMER

Emily Mortimer is the British actress who, in *Scream 3*, plays actress Angelina Tyler who plays Sidney Prescott in *Stab 3*. The daughter of the writer John Mortimer, she studied English and Russian at Lincoln College, Oxford, before turning to acting. After several appearances on British TV, beginning with Catherine Cookson's *The*

Glass Virgin in 1995, she made the transition to films with a role in *The Ghost and the Darkness* in 1996. Since then she's had roles in *The Saint*, *Elizabeth* and *Notting Hill*. *Scream 3* is Mortimer's first American film.

CARRIE FISHER

Carrie Fisher, who appears in *Scream 3*, was rumoured to be in *Scream 2* and said at the time, 'I have no ambitions to be an actress. I'm going to do a day's work on *Scream 2*, but that's all I can handle, a day's work.' In the event, she didn't even manage a day's work on that movie, but in *Scream 3* she does have a cameo as former actress Bianca Burnette, now head archivist at Sunset Studio archives.

Fisher, daughter of Fifties star Debbie Reynolds, will always be linked with her *Star Wars* role as Princess Leia, an association that has proved more of a curse than a blessing in terms of her acting career. Since *Star Wars* her filmography contains more lows than highs – like the embarrassing Australian-made sci-fi movie, *Time Guardian* (1987), *Amazon Women on the Moon* (1987) and *Drop Dead Fred* (1991).

Fishers, however, has had more success as a writer. Her first book, the autobiographical *Postcards from the Edge*, which concerned her drug-dependency days and her relationship with her overpowering mother, was filmed with Shirley MacLaine playing a thinly-disguised Debbie Reynolds and Meryl Streep playing Fisher herself. Fisher also has an uncredited cameo in the movie.

Among its many razor-sharp one-liners is this one delivered by Streep/Fisher, which sounds like the voice of experience: 'The trouble with instant gratification is that it's not fast enough.'

THE PLOT

The film begins with an aerial shot of the famous 'Hollywood' hill-side sign, which establishes the Hollywood setting of *Scream 3*. Cotton Weary (Liev Schreiber), stuck in traffic, receives a call on his cellphone from a mystery woman. Then the voice changes to that of a man who tells Cotton that he's watching Cotton's girlfriend, Kristine (Kelly Rutherford) and that he would kill to know where Sidney Prescott is. Cotton insists he doesn't know but the mystery caller isn't satisfied with this.

As Cotton drives furiously across Hollywood towards the apartment he shares with Kristine, she is already being stalked by Ghostface. She then receives a threatening phone call from, as she thinks, Cotton. In a gimmick new to *Scream 3* the killer possesses an electronic device which allows him to perfectly mimic other people's voices. So when Cotton arrives at the apartment, Kristine tries to knock him unconscious. And then Ghostface strikes – and both Cotton and Kristine are stabbed to death.

Sidney Prescott (Neve Campbell) is now living in a ranch house, in northern California, which is fitted with all manner of security devices. She lives alone, apart from an Irish setter (one automatically assumes the dog won't survive the movie but, surprisingly, it does). She works from her home, doing telephone crisis counselling for women, under the name of Laura.

We first see Gale Weathers (Courteney Cox Arquette) giving a lecture at a college. Gale is enjoying her new fame as anchorwoman on *Entertainment Tonight* (though we later learn that she had a much more prestigious job on *60 Minutes* but had been fired). She is then approached by LAPD homicide detective Mark Kincaid (Patrick Dempsey) who works for the Hollywood Division and is investigating the murders of Cotton and his girlfriend. The killer has left a 25-year-old photograph of Maurine Prescott (Linda McCree), Sidney's dead mother, on Cotton's body. Kincaid has rightly deduced that Cotton's death is linked to the famous Woodsboro Murders...

The action switches to Sunset Studios, where the latest movie about the Woodsboro Murders, *Stab 3*, is currently being shot. Roger Corman is the head of the studio, John Milton (Lance Henriksen) is the producer and the director is Roman Bridger (Scott Foley). Everyone is upset over Cotton's murder (he was due to have played a cameo in the movie), especially the apparently sweet and innocent young actress playing Sidney, Angelina Tyler (Emily Mortimer), and Jennifer Jolie (Parker Posey).

The real Gale Weathers turns up on the sound stage, having been given permission by Detective Kincaid to snoop around. Gale is surprised to run into her former boyfriend, Dewey Riley (David Arquette) who is working on the movie as a technical adviser. And she is less than pleased to meet her doppelganger, Jennifer, who Dewey is clearly smitten with. Then, when she is discovered by John Milton, Gale is ejected from the set (at this point Kevin Smith and Jason Mewes, as Silent Bob and Jay, have their cameo appearances as part of a group being given a tour of the studio).

At her remote hideaway, Sidney has a visitor, her father (Lawrence Hecht), who is trying to persuade her to return to Woodsboro. She refuses and he leaves. Sidney then has a vision of her dead mother wandering about the property. Her mother then talks to Sidney through the bedroom window, telling her, 'Everything you touch, dies. You're just like me.' Then she drops out of sight and Ghostface suddenly replaces her at the window, much to Sidney's horror. Then she wakes up. It had all been a dream...

At the studio, actress Sarah Darling (Jenny McCarthy) has arrived to discuss her small role in *Stab 3* as one of Ghostface's victims, with director Roman Bridger. He's not there, but then contacts her by phone. He tells her he wants her death scene to be shot in a shower but she responds with, 'The shower thing has been done. In *Vertigo*. Hello?' Then 'Roman's' voice changes into that of the killer and he threatens her. She flees and hides in a room in the costume department – which is full of Ghostface costumes suspended on hangers. One of them, of course, is inhabited by the real killer. After the classic *Scream*-style chase involving Ghostface and potential victim, he catches up with her and stabs her to death.

After the second murder the people at the film studio realize that the murders are being committed in the same order as the characters die in the screenplay for *Stab 3*, which is really upsetting for Jennifer Jolie as, according to the script, she's next in line. She becomes so upset that she leaps into the arms of her security guard, the insolent but very large Steven Stone (Patrick Warburton).

Back at the ranch, Sidney gets a phone call on her crisis line from someone who calls herself Linda who says she needs help because she's killed someone – then the voice changes into that of the killer...

Meanwhile, snooping as usual, Gale Weathers is hanging around Jennifer's Hollywood Hills home where Dewey lives in a trailer on the property (he and Jennifer have apparently been having an affair). While eavesdropping on Jennifer and Dewey (Angelina and an utterly superfluous character called Tony are also present), Gale is apprehended by Steven Stone who takes her into the house. Gale then reveals to Dewey, Jennifer and the others that she and Kincaid have discovered that Maurine Prescott disappeared from Woodsboro for two years before returning and marrying Sidney's father.

At the same time Stone is doing some snooping of his own – in Dewey's trailer. Then he gets a call on his cellphone from – he thinks – Dewey (who Stone insists on calling 'Dew Drop'). Of course, it's not the real Dewey but the killer using his electronic voice imitator. Ghostface appears, stabs Stone, then smashes him over the head with a frying pan. The others in the house are shocked when they see Stone stagger up the driveway and drop dead outside the front door. Then the lights go out.

The killer then starts faxing them revised pages of the *Stab 3* screenplay, adapted to describe their current, perilous, situation.

They all rush out of the house but Tony, who's very drunk, hears the fax machine being activated and returns to read the latest fax, which says that the killer will show mercy to whoever 'smells the gas'. However Tony has to flick his lighter on to read this vital piece of information and the house promptly blows up, killing him. The others are all blown over the fence and are sent tumbling down the hill to the road below.

Ghostface appears and almost succeeds in stabbing Gale. Dewey fires at him with his gun and Ghostface, seemingly unharmed, scuttles under a car and disappears. Then a very annoyed Jennifer accuses Dewey of paying Gale attention instead of her. Gale punches her out (a clever reference to when she was punched out by Sidney in the first two *Scream*s).

At long last, Sidney arrives in Hollywood, having decided that as the killer now knows where she lives she might as well join her few (very few) surviving friends. She turns up the Hollywood police station where she meets Detective Kincaid and it's immediately obvious that the two of them are interested in each other. In a badly handled attempt at a red herring, Kincaid is painted as a potential suspect by the fact that he has posters from *Murders in the Rue Morgue* and *Kiss Me Deadly* on his wall. Even more ominously, he has books about the movies on his shelves and later we learn that he knows his way around the studios and regards Hollywood as 'death'. All of which suggest to any self-respecting *Scream* fan that he can be completely ruled out as a serious suspect.

In a cameo scene, Heather Matarazzo (*Welcome to the Dollhouse*), turns up as Martha Meeks, the dead Randy's sister. She has a videotape in her possession made by Randy which he left to be played in the event of his death. In the video he warns, among other things, that they are not in a sequel but in the third part of a trilogy, which have rules all of their own; that the killer will be superhuman and anyone in the cast can die, including lead characters.

Since the photographs of Maurine Roberts (as she then was) left by the bodies of the victims look like studio stills, Jennifer and Gale team up to snoop around the Sunset Studio archives. The head of the archives is a chain-smoking, former actress called Bianca Burnette who is tired of being told she looks like Carrie Fisher (it is, naturally, Carrie Fisher doing a cameo). Jennifer bribes her into revealing that 25 years ago John Milton made three horror films starring Sidney's mom, who in those days went under the name of Reena Reynolds.

Meanwhile Sidney, wandering about the studio, discovers the seemingly angelic Angelina donning a Ghostface costume in a toilet cubicle. Angelina protests that she was just helping herself to one of the costumes because the *Stab 3* production has been shut down (due to an increasingly shortage of actors) but Sidney isn't buying it. Alarmed, Angelina flees onto the darkened *Stab 3* sound stage. Sidney follows her – and is stunned when she finds herself on a set that is a perfect reproduction of the house she grew up in. Sitting on 'her' bed in 'her' bedroom, she starts having flashbacks to *Scream* and then Ghostface turns up for real.

There follows yet another of those typical Ghostface/victim chases, with Ghostface managing to fall over practically anything it's possible to fall over/collide with while chasing Sidney upstairs. But, as it's just a film set, Sidney discovers that a door she's about to flee through opens onto thin air. She recovers in time to yank Ghostface through it and he sails into space, falling onto 'her' bed on the set below. Then Dewey, Gale, Kincaid and the others enter the sound stage, turning on the lights. Ghostface has disappeared and, inexplicably, nobody believes Sidney when she insists he was there...

While Sidney and Kincaid head back to the police station, Dewey, Gale and Jennifer confront John Milton in his office, which is full of horror props. Milton has just been having an argument with director Roman Bridger. After Bridger leaves to attend his own birthday party being held at Milton's Hollywood Hills mansion, Milton confesses to the others that he did know Reena Reynolds (aka Sidney's mom) and that something bad, of a sexual nature, happened to her at that time which is why she left Hollywood.

Later Dewey, in his car with the others, gets a call on his cellphone from Sidney. She tells them to come at once to Milton's house where she'll meet them with Kincaid. Of course, the call is not really from Sidney. At the party our band of heroes decide to split into pairs to search the house. It transpires that the house is full of secret rooms where Milton used to show porno films. Roman goes down to the basement, which is full of props, leaving Jennifer fretting at the top of the stairs. Meanwhile, Gale and Dewey have had the bright idea of calling back the last number on Dewey's phone (the bogus Sidney call) and then hear a phone ringing in the house. They track it down and find, with the phone, the voice-imitating electronic gadget... and a Ghostface mask.

Later, in the basement Gale finds Roman lying in a coffin with a knife in his chest. She meets up with Jennifer and they then encounter a distraught Angelina who, we learn, has slept with Milton to get the part in the movie. She unwisely rushes off on her own and encounters Ghostface who then kills her. Jennifer, meanwhile, has also unwisely wandered off on her own and finds herself in an area which has a series of windows on her side, but which are mirrors on the side where Gale and Dewey are prowling about. They, for some reason, can't hear her when she bangs on the glass. Then Ghostface appears again. When he attacks Jennifer, Dewey wakes up and starts shooting out the mirror/windows, but it's too late...A fight between Dewey, Gale and Ghostface follows, and they all end up falling into the cellar...

At the police station, Sidney gets a call from the killer, who tells her that he's holding Dewey and Gale captive and that he'll kill them unless she comes to Milton's house. Before leaving the station Sidney 'borrows' a gun (or two, as it later turns out) and the car keys belonging to a detective's vehicle. At the Milton mansion, after being obliged to throw her gun away, she attempts to free Gale and Dewey but Ghostface appears. Sidney produces the second gun, from nowhere, and shoots him. But, as Randy had predicted, Ghostface now appears to be superhuman because he promptly disappears.

Kincaid shows up at the house but is attacked by Ghostface and knocked out. Fleeing, Sidney goes through a hidden door and finds herself in a very elaborate room. And, of course, Ghostface appears, confronts her – and removes his mask. It is revealed that Ghosface is none other than the director, Roman Bridger (who could have guessed?) who's been wearing a bullet-proof vest the whole time!

It turns out that when Sidney's mom was in Hollywood, she went to a party at Milton's house and had sex, or was raped, in the very room that Sidney is now in. Roman was conceived as a result. Rejected by his mother, young Roman grew up bitter and twisted. But somehow he tracked her to Woodsboro and confronted her. She again rejected him. Becoming even more bitter and twisted, if that's possible, he secretly filmed some of her affairs, including the one with Billy Loomis's father. After showing the film to Billy, he convinced Billy to murder Sidney's mother.

Meanwhile Dewey and Gale, having got free, are trying to break into the secret room. In said room Roman hauls a bound-and-gagged John Milton out of a closet. Roman rips the gaffer tape from his mouth and the terrified Milton offers him any deal he wants, even the 'final cut' of the movie. Roman says he has his own final cut in mind, and slashes Milton's throat. Roman then tells Sidney that his plan is to use his voice gadget to leave a message from 'Sidney' on Milton's answer machine explaining how she killed everyone and then shot herself.

A climatic fight develops. Kincaid blunders in, but to little effect (much of his role has been to little effect). Roman shoots Sidney but she temporarily disappears, then reappears to stab him with an ice pick. She reveals that she too is wearing a bullet-proof vest (as they're related it must be genetic). She then stabs Roman with his own knife, and holds his hand while he dies. Finally Dewey and Gale enter the room but, lo and behold, Roman suddenly comes back to life! Was Randy right after all? Dewey shoots at him but that damn bullet-proof vest is still working. Sidney wisely suggests to Dewey that he aim at Roman's head. Dewey does so and Roman expires.

In the epilogue, which takes place at Sidney's ranch house, Dewey proposes to Gale (ahhh!). Kincaid is also there and when Sidney returns from a walk with her dog, he invites her into the living room to watch a movie (not *Scream*). As she does so the front door blows open but she doesn't even flinch.

CREDITS

Director	Wes Craven
Screenplay	Ehren Kruger
Cinematographer	Peter Deming
Original Music	Marco Beltrami
Producers	Cathy Konrad, Marianne Maddalena
Executive Producers	Bob Weinstein
	Harvey Weinstein
	Andrew Rona

CAST

Dwight 'Dewey' Riley . . . . David Arquette

Sidney Prescott . . . . Neve Campbell

Gale Weathers (as Courtney Cox Arquette). . . . . . . Courteney Cox

Detective Mark Kincaid. . . . . Patrick Dempsey

Roman Bridger . . . . Scott Foley

John Milton . . . . Lance Henriksen

Tom Prinze. . . . . Matthew Keeslar

Sarah Darling/Tatum in *Stab 3* . . . . Jenny McCarthy

Angelina Tyler/Sidney in *Stab 3* . . . . Emily Mortimer

Jennifer Jolie/Gale in *Stab 3* . . . . Parker Posey

Gabe Tucker/Joel in *Stab 3* . . . . Deon Richmond

Bianca Burnette. . . . . Carrie Fisher

Phone Voice (voice). Roger L. Jackson

Kristine. . . . . Kelly Rutherford

Cotton Weary . . . . Liev Schreiber

KEVIN WILLIAMSON

THE MAN WHO WROTE *SCREAM*

When Kevin Williamson switched from being a struggling actor to being a struggling scriptwriter, it turned to be a very wise career move on his part. Not that he really wanted to become a struggling scriptwriter, or even a non-struggling one. His ultimate goal was to become a director, but he'd decided that scriptwriting offered a better chance of reaching this objective than acting – and he was right.

Williamson was born on 14 March 1965, in New Bern, North Carolina, not far from scenic Dawson's Creek. Williamson's father was a fisherman and the family was not exactly awash with money when he was growing up. They lived in a trailer next to a creek and, according to Williamson, 'If you called us white trash, we probably couldn't argue the point too well. We were like really classy white trash – we were happy about it.'

However, young Williamson dreamed of escape, and like so many others he found a temporary form of escape in movies. But unlike the majority of cinema fans, who are satisfied to remain passive consumers of celluloid fantasies, Williamson was of that particular type who is determined to put flesh on their movie fantasies by becoming *part* of the movie industry. So, naturally, Kevin Williamson decided to become a movie director...

His first step in the grand plan was to move to New York and become an actor. He did, but found himself playing small – tiny – parts in theatre and television: he got a small role in the long-running daytime soap opera *Another World* in 1990 and, in one of his few film roles, in a 1994 movie called *Dirty Money*, he was listed in the credits as 'Drunk American Guy'. In 1991 he hit rock bottom with no money and no prospects and the growing feeling that he'd be better off dead. If it hadn't been for a friend who kept him going by lending him money and paying his rent, Williamson doesn't like to think of what his fate might have been. But then he got some more acting work and, with the money, decided to move to LA in the hope that his luck might change for the better. In LA he worked as an assistant to a music video director and worked his way up to production manager, but he wasn't satisfied.

Having long given up on the hope of becoming even a moderately successful actor, he borrowed money from another friend and enrolled in a course on screenwriting at UCLA (the same university as his hero, Steven Spielberg, once attended). During the course he wrote a screenplay called *Killing Mrs Tingle*. 'It was a comedy about a young high school girl who is one point shy of becoming a valedictorian,' said Williamson. 'So she sets out to kill the English teacher responsible.' The central character of the teacher was based on a teacher he'd encountered during his high school days back in North Carolina. It was this real-life Mrs Tingle who'd stifled his teenage ambitions of becoming a writer. 'She tore me down. I read a story out loud in class and she told me to "Sit down, shut up." She told me I had a voice that shouldn't be heard. "Any dream you have about being a writer, just forget it. It'll never happen. You're too stupid." I was 15 at the time. I was so insecure about so many other issues I just thought, "Give up. Give up." After that I didn't believe I had any talent as a writer.'

But it was another incident involving this paragon of the teaching profession that provided Williamson with the core idea for *Killing Mrs Tingle*:

I was in the gym with some friends the last week of school, and I got caught doing something I wasn't supposed to be doing by this teacher. We went to her house that night and begged her forgiveness; begged her not to turn us in because it could ruin our futures. And she just slammed the door in our faces. And we went home and took our punishment. But in the screenplay I wrote, the revenge fantasy part is that they don't go home. When the door is slammed in their faces, they re-open it. And things go from bad to worse.

Williamson thought his struggling days were over when his screenplay was quickly snapped up: 'I gave it to a friend who had an agent, and two weeks later I was signed with the agent. We sold it to Interscope and Joe Dante was going to direct it. Joe was a great guy and he would have been the perfect director for it, but he left after we worked for almost a year on rewriting the script.' The project then became trapped in the usual 'development hell'. Williamson was even removed from his own screenplay and replaced by a team of other writers (one of whom was Trey Parker who later hit the big time with *South Park*). It became clear to him that nothing was going to happen with it in the immediate future.

It was during this hiatus that he wrote the screenplay called *Scary Movie*, which became the object of a bidding war among various major Hollywood players, was bought by the Dimension Films wing of Miramax for $500,000, and eventually became *Scream*. At the same time that they bought his screenplay Miramax offered him a three-picture deal, which he eagerly accepted. Kevin Williamson was up and running, and hasn't stopped since, though there have been some stumbles along the way.

While *Scream* was setting box-office records he signed up with Columbia Pictures to write *I Know What You Did Last Summer*, another pretty-teens-being-menaced-by-psycho-killer effort, but minus the post-modernist irony. It too made money but annoyed the bosses at Miramax, who especially objected to Columbia's use, in their advertising campaign, of the claim that the film was 'From the Creator of *Scream*': they hit Columbia with a lawsuit.

Columbia had approached Williamson with the project, which was based on a juvenile-adult novel by Lois Duncan. 'I really responded to the characters and their predicament,' said Williamson, 'because they make one wrong decision and it may cost them their lives. It appealed to me because it's similar to William Castle's *I Saw What You Did*, which I really liked, but it ended up more in the direction of *Friday the 13th*, except it's smarter.' All he took from the original novel, written in the 1970s, was the basic premise of the four teenagers being involved in a hit-and-run fatality and the consequences when they attempt to cover up their crime:

> *I just didn't think the novel was at all cinematic. Once you find out who the killer is in the book, you know it would never work translated into film terms. I upped the stakes, added more characters, and the villain. I changed the setting to a North Carolina fishing village, just like the one I grew up in. It made it more personal and more interesting to me. So then the villain became a fisherman. My Dad is a fisherman and I thought this would be a great homage to my Dad – he'll really enjoy this. Then I got to use all my knowledge of fishing trawlers to create scary moments.*

After writing *Scream 2*, Williamson contributed to the script for *Halloween H20* (US title: *Halloween H20: Twenty Years Later*), a project he was reluctant to become involved with despite his love of the original *Halloween* film. 'My initial response was, "Don't talk to me about it",' he told *Starburst* magazine, 'because I thought they'd killed the series with the last one [*Halloween: The Curse of Michael Myers*].' But when he was working on his TV series *Dawson's Creek*, on location in North Carolina, he was introduced to Jamie Lee Curtis.

> *She was there shooting* Virus *and the first thing she said to me was, 'We're making* Halloween H20 *twenty years later. It's got to happen right now for the twentieth anniversary!' And she started pitching me the trailer: 'Just imagine a dark screen and a voice says 'Twenty years ago...' Then all of a sudden you hear the* Halloween *theme.' I just went, 'Yeah!'*

After that I made a few phone calls and I was in. But the only reason I'm part of H20 is because of Jamie.

Williamson declined to take a credit for his work on the screenplay, though he is credited as one of the executive producers.

Miramax, hoping for a new horror franchise to rival that of the *Scream* movies, persuaded him to write *The Faculty* for them, with the added inducement that he would have the opportunity to direct it. In the end, however, his other commitments prevented him from doing so, and it was directed by Robert Rodriguez. Williamson described *The Faculty* as a 'sort of homage to *Invasion of the Bodysnatchers*', which it is, but it also incorporates the same theme that fuels *Killing Mrs Tingle*, and one close to his heart – that high school teachers aren't to be trusted.

His directing debut was to be on *Killing Mrs Tingle* (the title was changed to *Teaching Mrs Tingle* by Miramax, partly as a response to the Columbine High School tragedy), an experience he found extremely enjoyable. He told *Fade In* magazine, 'I had been waiting my whole life to direct a film and I loved it. I was walking on clouds throughout the shooting. It was so much fun – it wasn't nearly as hard as everyone made it out to be.' He also enjoyed working with his star, Helen Mirren, who played Mrs Tingle. 'I was so nervous about working with a star of that calibre but she was wonderful and we just clicked from the very beginning. She was so amazing.'

Unfortunately, the reception that *Teaching Mrs Tingle* received on its release in the middle of 1999, from both the critics and the audience, was a far from pleasurable experience for Williamson. On the contrary, it was the first serious setback in what had appeared to be an unstoppable upward career climb since *Scream*. *Teaching Mrs Tingle* wasn't helped by the fact that it was bringing up the rear in a whole landslide of teen movies set around high schools – including *She's All That, Cruel Intentions, Never Been Kissed, Varsity Blues, American Pie, Ten Things I Hate About You, Election* and *Rushmore* – but the general consensus was that Williamson's contribution to the genre was well below par. And as the director as well as the scriptwriter, he was attacked on two fronts at once.

And 1999 saw another setback to his alternative career – the one in television. In 1998 he'd launched a teenage soap opera called *Dawson's Creek*, an autobiographical series set in North Carolina, where Williamson grew up. The show's hero, Dawson (James Van Der Beek), is a student film-maker, and his speech is peppered with movie references, not dissimilar to those of a character in a *Scream* film (and each episode of the series is named after a well-known movie). It was a popular success and Williamson was encouraged to make another series, this one aimed at an older audience for a prime-time TV slot. Called *Wasteland*, and starring Rebecca Gayheart from *Scream 2*, it was also part of his multi-million-dollar deal with Miramax and represented the company's first venture into television. So both Williamson and Miramax had a lot riding on the show. Set in New York, and once again autobiographical, it drew upon Williamson's experiences in that city when he was struggling to survive. He said, 'With *Dawson's Creek* we were dealing with teenagers coming of age whereas with *Wasteland* the whole show is about that second coming of age as you approach thirty. It's sink or swim. And that's what all these characters are grappling with. It's rife with conflict, which makes a weekly show.'

When *Wasteland* was aired, however, the critics were not kind. One wrote: 'Like *Dawson's Creek*, it is about a group of people who won't stop analysing themselves,' while in *Vanity Fair* James Wolcott said:

> *Despite its stark title,* Wasteland *is a cocktail of* Friends, Felicity, Ally McBeal *and* Sex and the City; *an ensemble dramedy about a daisy chain of twenty-somethings whose lives jostle and collide like lottery balls in pressure-cooker Manhattan. As if trained at the Quentin Tarantino/Kevin Smith school of rapid reciting, some of the characters speed through their monologues like drag racers burning rubber... The urban adrenaline is thinned out, however, by a cast that is a standard bouquet of pretty things, so generically, unselfconsciously hip-young-now that they seem stuck in a revolving door at the Gap... The guys are the real ingenues here.*

Dawson's Creek made James Van Der Beek a gay icon... and Wasteland is even more homoerotic. A gratuitous yet invigorating shower scene between two former college studs (one of whom comes out of the closet under the faucet) showcases such buff physiques and toreador towel action that the cast of NYPD Blue may be shamed into doing special clenching exercises if they intend to compete in the butt-shot department.

The audience ratings reflected the less-than-impressed reactions of the critics and the show was 'temporarily' taken off the air after only a short run.

Kevin Williamson has repeatedly stated that he doesn't want to be typecast as a horror specialist – in fact, he was warned against the dangers of being 'pegged as a horror guy' by none other than Wes Craven – which is why he moved into non-horror areas such as *Dawson's Creek* and *Wasteland*. And the next feature film he plans to direct is a romantic comedy, *Her Leading Man*, about a young woman who has her faith in true love restored by a bitter out-of-work screenwriter (the autobiographical element is again more than obvious). But the signs are that he might need *Scream 3* to be as successful as the first two in the series in order to remind people in the industry of his once-golden, sure-fire, touch. This is despite the fact that Williamson didn't write the screenplay of *Scream 3* – nor was his story treatment used (the story and script was written by Ehren Kruger, who wrote the screenplay for the thriller, *Arlington Road*). Williamson was too busy with his *Wasteland* project to be more fully involved with the movie – though, ironically, both productions ended up being filmed in the same studio and Williamson was able to wander over from the set of *Wasteland* to visit his friends on the set of *Scream 3*.

'Everything has been a calculated career move from the very, very beginning,' Williamson now claims.

Certainly anybody who knows my career knows what a big Steven Spielberg fan I am. They know that from Dawson's Creek. *I've read his biography; I've watched all of his career.*

I was filming movies in my backyard when I was ten, just like he did, with an 8mm camera. I just wanted it so badly. And then, after Scream... *Wes Craven drilled it into my brain that you're going to be pegged as a horror guy, so make sure you don't follow* Scream *up with any horror movies. Well, I made the mistake. I followed it up with* I Know What You Did Last Summer, The Faculty *and* Halloween H2O... *I love romantic comedies. I love movies like* Terms of Endearment, When Harry Met Sally... *and* Jerry Maguire. *That's the stuff I want to make, that's the stuff I'm passionate about. That's the stuff I do best.*

Williamson may be anxious to leave the world of horror films behind him but, as his mentor, Wes Craven, has found out, once you've made your name, and your bed, in the horror genre, it's hard to escape its clutches when you feel it's time to say farewell and move on.

THE FACULTY (1998)

Directed by **Robert Rodriguez**, screenplay by **Kevin Williamson, David Wechter** and **Bruce Kimmel**. Starring **Jordana Brewster, Clea Du Vall, Laura Harris, Josh Hartnett, Shawn Hatosy, Salma Hayek, Famke Janssen, Piper Laurie, Bebe Neuwirth, Robert Patrick.**

With *The Faculty*, Williamson gave the *Scream* treatment to science fiction movies, specifically *Invasion of the Bodysnatchers* and *The Thing*, while adding to the mix a large dollop of John Hughes' influential teen movie, *The Breakfast Club*, as well as the theme from his own *Teaching Mrs Tingle* – that high school teachers are Bad News.

When the teaching staff of a high school in Ohio are taken over by aliens it falls to an uneasy alliance of six dysfunctional students to save the school, the town and possibly the entire world from alien domination. (Actually the whole school is pretty dysfunctional even before the alien invasion – unlike the pristine middle-class establishments that usually feature in these high school movies, this one is refreshingly sleazy.) As with *Scream*, it's the exhaustive knowledge that some of the characters have about films, in this case SF/horror movies, that allows them to fight back. And not just movies – classic SF novels are also referred to and one character, Stokely (Clea Du Vall), is actually seen *reading* a novel (by Robert Heinlein). Acting on the assumption that the aliens themselves must follow the rules of the genre, the gang of six concentrate on finding, and killing, the key alien who controls all the others (though in what alien invasion film this 'rule' was established isn't made clear). Needless to say, after various setbacks, the teens are victorious.

It's all a great deal of fun and Robert Rodriguez (*El Mariachi, From Dusk till Dawn*) directs with panache. The younger cast members are fine but, ironically, are no match in the acting stakes for the older actors playing the teachers (including Bebe Neuwirth, Famke Janssen and Robert Patrick – Schwarzenegger's opponent in *Terminator 2*), with the result that you end up wishing that the film spent more time with the possessed teachers than the rebel students.

HALLOWEEN H20 (1998)

Directed by **Steve Miner**, screenplay by **Robert Zappia** and **Matt Greenberg** (and **Kevin Williamson**, uncredited). Starring **Jamie Lee Curtis, Adam Arkin, Josh Hartnett, Michelle Williams, Adam Hann-Byrd, Jodi Lyn O'Keefe, LL Cool J, Janet Leigh**.

Kevin Williamson seems to have distanced himself from this belated sequel to *Halloween*, and though he did contribute to the screenplay, he didn't take a screenwriting credit (though he is credited as being one of the executive producers). As the producers of the *Scream* movies, Bob and Harvey Weinstein, were also involved, it's clear that someone at Miramax thought it would be a great idea to have Williamson involved with a sequel to the very movie that inspired him to write *Scream* – particularly as the original star, Jamie Lee Curtis, had agreed to participate.

There were six previous *Halloween* movies but *Halloween H2O* follows on from the second in the series and ignores the events of the last four. Twenty years on, Jamie Lee's character, Laurie Strode, is living under a new name, Kari Tate, having faked her own death some years previously. She now runs a private school in northern California and has a 17-year-old son, John. She also has a drinking problem and suffers from nightmares about her homicidal brother, Michael. And, to add to her woes, her least favourite time of the year, Halloween, is just around the corner... as, of course, is Michael, who has finally tracked her down.

The build-up is handled well, as is Jamie Lee Curtis's portrait of a woman approaching middle age and saddled not only with the usual problems of a single mother, coping with a rebellious teenage son, but also with a patronizing lover, alcoholism, the running of an entire school and a family skeleton that insists on repeatedly coming out of the closet. But once Michael turns up, just as the students are holding a Halloween party, and the mayhem gets under way, the film follows a predictable path and genuine shocks are thin on the ground. It's only at the end, when ingenious play is made of Michael's traditional tendency to keep coming back to life, that the film itself stirs into life to deliver a nail-biting climax. Along the way, naturally, there are the usual movie in-jokes and references that are Williamson's trademarks. The best of these is in a sequence which features Janet Leigh – the star of *Psycho* and mother of Jamie Lee. As screen and real-life mother and daughter do their scene together, a snatch of Bernard Herrmann's famous score for *Psycho* is briefly heard on the soundtrack.

I KNOW WHAT YOU DID LAST SUMMER (1997)

Directed by **Jim Gillespie**, screenplay by **Kevin Williamson** (based on the novel by **Lois Duncan**). Starring **Jennifer Love Hewitt, Sarah Michelle Gellar, Ryan Phillipe, Freddie Prinze Jr., Muse Watson, Bridgette Wilson, Anne Heche.**

Between *Scream*s Kevin Williamson wrote the screenplay for this okay but average horror movie that definitely lacks the innovative sparkle of *Scream*. Eschewing all the post-modernistic ironies of *Scream*, it's a straightforward psycho-killer-on-the-loose story of the kind that Williamson was sending up in his first movie.

Four teenagers in their car hit and apparently kill a man after a drunken party. They dump the body in the sea but the following year they start receiving notes from someone who claims to know what they did. Is it possible their victim is still alive? And then the murders start – and it all becomes too predictable. On the plus side, the fishing village setting, based on Williamson's first-hand experiences of growing up in such a town, adds a novelty value, as well as an element of verisimilitude, to the background. Williamson is also good at deftly establishing the class tensions in the community, another touch of realism that is rare in a genre film such as this. Also good value are the attractive young cast who, like the cast of *Scream*, were drawn mainly from television. The lead actress, Jennifer Love Hewitt, was appearing in the same TV show as *Scream*'s heroine, Neve Campbell – the popular *Party of Five*. And, at the time of the shooting of the film, Sarah Michelle Gellar was waiting anxiously to hear how her new TV series, *Buffy the Vampire Slayer*, was doing in the ratings.

I Know What You Did Last Summer adequately delivers the required number of thrills and chills but, as directed by Jim Gillespie (whose only previous directing credit was on the 1995 TV series *The Ghostbusters of East Finchley*), it remains a pedestrian effort and highlights just how much horror maestro Wes Craven brought to the collaboration on *Scream*. Wisely, Williamson declined to be involved in the sequel, *I Still Know What You Did Last Summer*, written by Trey Callaway and directed by Danny (*Judge Dredd*) Cannon, which turned out to be a truly dismal piece of horror cinema.

TEACHING MRS TINGLE (1999)

Directed by **Kevin Williamson**, screenplay by **Kevin Williamson**. Starring **Katie Holmes**, **Helen Mirren**, **Marisa Coughlan**, **Liz Stauber**, **Jeffrey Tambor**, **Lesley Ann Warren**.

Originally called *Killing Mrs Tingle*, this film marked Kevin Williamson's directing debut and is based on his first, strongly auto-biographical, screenplay. Katie Holmes (from *Dawson's Creek*), playing Williamson's (female) *alter ego*, Leigh Anne Warren, is a high school student wrongly accused of cheating by the teacher-from-hell, Mrs Tingle (Helen Mirren) just days before graduation. Leigh and two of her friends, Jo Lynn and Luke (Marisa Coughlan, who later appeared in Williamson's *Wasteland* TV series, and Barry Watson), pay a visit to Mrs Tingle at her home to plead with her to change her mind. When the teacher refuses, they force their way into the house and, after a struggle, Mrs Tingle ends up tied to her bed – a hostage. A war of nerves follows, ending with the predictable outbreak of violence.

Helen Mirren is the best thing in *Teaching Mrs Tingle*, her icy portrayal suggesting that Mrs Tingle is an escapee from Williamson's other foray into secondary school education – the much more enter-taining *The Faculty*. The rest of the cast, in particular Marisa Coughlan, are fine, given the limitations of the script, which does not rate as one of Williamson's better efforts. Basically there's not much entertainment to be derived from this resolutely unexciting psychological thriller and one can't help comparing it unfavourably with other films with similar themes (*Misery*, *Suicide Kings* and *Swimming with Sharks*). Unfortunately, Williamson's first film as a director suggests that his undoubted talent as a scriptwriter hasn't yet translated into an equal facility for directing. As Mrs Tingle would have written on his report card – Must Do Better.

GETTING TO THE GUTS OF WES CRAVEN

Wes Craven has only himself to blame for his success. Here he is, America's top horror movie director, but he has repeatedly complained that he is unhappy at being pigeonholed in the horror genre and has made several determined attempts to escape his typecasting. His latest attempt was his last movie, *Music of the Heart*, as far away from horror as you can get (unless your idea of horror is a film where Meryl Streep gives violin lessons to under-privileged kids in Harlem), and he recently published his first novel, *The Fountain Society*, a medical thriller with science fiction overtones, and described by one reviewer as '...sheer 100% tosh...but Craven's pacy, assured prose style, lively dialogue and dark humour keep things engrossing in the initial stages...until the plot gets too ridiculous for anything to rescue it.' And now, with his third *Scream* movie completed, he is once again expressing his desire to lay down his bloodstained sceptre. 'I don't think it's going to be my last genre picture,' he said on the set of *Scream 3*, 'but I'd like to think it will be my last film where somebody is chasing somebody else around with a knife. If something like *The Sixth Sense* came up, I wouldn't mind doing that. But I don't really feel like I want to do more of this.'

Ah, yes, *The Sixth Sense* – which, in 1999, knocked the first two *Scream* movies off their perch by claiming their previously-held box-office record as the most successful horror film (with *The Blair Witch Project* coming up in second place). But it's not just the financial success of *The Sixth Sense* that must be niggling at Craven; it's also the knowledge that the director of *The Sixth Sense*, M. Night Shyamalan, is not going to be branded as a sleazy purveyor of blood and gore who is corrupting the youth of America. Ever since Craven arrived on the film scene with his breakthrough movie, the blood-stained and gut-strewn *Last House on the Left* in 1972, he's been having to live with this label and, understandably, he's getting more than a little weary of it.

Wes Craven gave no indication in his early years that he was destined to become America's foremost horror director, never mind a purveyor of corrupting movie imagery. He was born in Cleveland, Ohio, in 1939, and grew up in a very strict environment, his working-class family being devout fundamentalist Baptists. Because of his family's religious beliefs, his cinema-going was severely restricted during his childhood and he was only introduced to the cinema when he left home to attend college. The films he saw in college were mainly by European film-makers such as Buñuel, Fellini, Bergman and Cocteau. In this he shares a strikingly similar background with writer–director Paul Schrader, who was brought up in a strict Calvinist family and prevented from seeing any movies during his formative years. Schrader too had to wait until he attended university, at UCLA, before he was introduced to the cinema. He then became a film critic, producing academic papers on European and Japanese film-makers, before writing the screenplays for *The Yakuza* and *Taxi Driver*, and then directing *Hard Core*, *American Gigolo* and *Cat People*. Clearly, being raised in an atmosphere of religious repression, banned from seeing any movies during your formative years, has an odd effect on people.

Craven has no doubts that the circumstances of his childhood had a detrimental effect on him psychologically:

> *I came from a broken home with a father who was pretty scary [his father died when he was five]. I was raised in a very fundamentalist family, with all that sort of hellfire and*

brimstone preaching, and I think those kind of things affected me. Telling a little kid he's going to burn in hell forever – that's a pretty scary concept. It was a complete immersion in religion, surrounded by people who believe so deeply in something you can't quite believe. It's a lifelong thing, repairing your head.

At Wheaton University, where Billy Graham had once been a student, Craven became editor of the college magazine and published articles questioning the Baptist faith. This led to him receiving his first taste of the censors' wrath that was to become a familiar fixture in his life. He was denounced from the pulpit and the magazine was suspended.

Craven then obtained a Masters degree in Philosophy from John Hopkins University, and after leaving college he became a teacher, lecturing in English and the humanities. He married in 1964 and a couple of years later moved, with his wife and two children, to New York state, where he took up a teaching post at Clarkson College. But by now the academic life was beginning to pall and, after making an amateur film with some of his students at Clarkson, he decided, like so many others in 1968, to drop out. He had had his epiphany – he was going to become a film-maker.

He moved to New York City and began looking for work in the film industry. He made some potentially useful contacts but none of these led to any work, so he was obliged to return to teaching for a year at a local high school. In 1969 he linked up with a former student from Clarkson, Harry Chapin, who'd become an editor on TV commercials and documentaries. While hanging around on the fringes of the film industry, Craven supported his family by working in the sort of jobs that look interesting on a CV once you've become a success but are not much fun at the time – he swept floors, was a messenger and drove a cab for six months. During this period he was also picking up valuable skills, such as editing, from the bunch of underground film-makers he'd met through Chapin. But none of this made him much money and, not surprisingly, his marriage collapsed. Even so, he still had to provide an income for his two children and his financial situation was growing increasingly desperate. It was now 1971, he was 31, and his future looked bleak. And then he met a fledgling film producer by the name of Sean S. Cunningham, an encounter that was to have a profound effect on Craven's life and career.

He worked with Cunningham on an underground movie called *Together*, and when the company that financed it, the Hallmark Releasing Corporation, asked Cunningham and Craven to come up with an idea for a cheap, 'no-holds-barred horror movie', Cunningham asked Craven if he would like to write, direct and edit it. Craven said, 'Sure,' even though he wasn't at all familiar with the horror genre. All he knew was that a horror film was supposed to scare people. He wrote the script over a weekend while staying with friends in Long Island and called it *Sex Crime of the Century*. The title was later changed to *Last House on the Left*. This notorious movie would kick-start Craven's career as a director, but it would also label him as a horror director and, in some people's minds, a weird sicko…

Based, very loosely, on Ingmar Bergman's *The Virgin Spring*, *Last House on the Left* concerns three escaped psychopaths, and the girl-friend of their leader, Krug, who abduct two teenage girls, then torture, rape and kill them. Later, the four end up at the home of the parents of one of the dead girls, posing as stranded travellers. When the parents discover the truth, they exact a bloody revenge on the four, which involves throat-slitting, castration and a chainsaw. The plot may have been similar to Bergman's film but where Craven's version differed radically was in his decision to show the violence in extremely graphic detail, in particular, a disembowelling scene that many found especially shocking.

'I felt it very strongly and I needed to get it out of my system,' said Craven. 'I've never felt the need to go that far again. I've never felt it was necessary to make that explicit statement about violence again. I mean, I could only watch that picture a few times. It's not a picture to be looked at over and over again and enjoyed.' Craven also remains sensitive about a protracted rape sequence: 'I felt like that's enough. I've done it once and I don't ever want to be in any sense glamorizing rape and making it look like an interesting or dramatic device. It's such a touchy area, something that's been done so much in movies. I do shy away from that.'

But Hallmark were happy with the finished picture and, after Sean Cunningham had made some cuts in the violence to appease the MPAA, they released it in their chain of cinemas under the title *Krug and Company* in July 1972. Then Hallmark relaunched it in August that year with the title *Last House on the Left*, a change Craven wasn't happy with. 'I still think it's a nothing title,' he said. 'There's no last house on the left in the movie. But it took off.'

And take off it did, slowly at first, and then, as it was released in more markets across America in late 1972 and at the start of 1973, it became a cult success. It also attracted reviews. A couple were favourable (the influential critic Roger Ebert liked it), but the majority were negative. Craven ruefully remembers that the words 'shameful', 'morbid' and 'repugnant' cropped up a lot. It also attracted the attention of various self-styled censors, despite having been given an 'R' certificate by the MPAA. '*Last House* was censored more or less ad hoc in the US by local groups and theatre managers,' said Craven. 'And even by projectionists. Everybody had a snip at it.'

In Britain, of course, it was promptly banned. And when it later turned up on video release in the UK, 104 courts found it obscene. *Last House on the Left*, along with *Driller Killer*, *Evil Dead*, *Cannibal Holocaust* and *I Spit on Your Grave*, became the hard core of titles targeted by the tabloid press, the National Viewers' and Listeners' Association and certain politicians in the campaign to have the so-called 'video nasties' banned. This led to the Video Recordings Act of 1984 that brought videos under the control of the British Board of Film Censors, giving that body even greater powers (and changing its name to the British Board of Film Classification in the process). Some of the 'video nasties' – including *Evil Dead* and *Driller Killer* – are now legally available on video in the UK, but it's very unlikely that *Last House* will ever get a certificate.

Craven also found that his connection with *Last House* was having an effect on his personal relationships. Certain friends and acquaintances began acting oddly in his presence: 'People literally wouldn't leave their children alone with me. They would get up and walk away from the table when I went out to have dinner. There was this powerful feeling that we had done something unspeakable.'

But, on the plus side, *Last House on the Left* was making money (costing $90,000 to make, *Last House* had grossed about $18 million by 1982), and some of it was actually coming Craven's way. In the first year after it was released he made nearly $100,000 and at last his decision to give up teaching began to look like a sensible one.

However, the success of the movie initially had no beneficial effects on his film-making career. On the contrary, it proved a hindrance. 'I was considered such a bad boy that nobody would entrust me with anything but a horror film. Sean Cunningham and I wrote about five films, all non-horror subjects, and nobody would talk to us. I didn't want to be a horror director. I just wanted to direct films. We had to go off and follow separate careers.' After moving to Los Angeles, Craven spent the next three years trying to get his own non-horror projects off the ground, but without any luck.

Craven started work as an editor again. One person he worked for was director Peter Locke, who said he should seriously consider making another horror film. If he did, Locke said he would produce it. At first Craven refused, but it was now five years since the success of *Last House*. Craven had exhausted his residual payments from the movie and was fast approaching 40. Once again his career seemed to be going nowhere, so he decided to take Locke's suggestion, and offer, seriously. He started writing a story for a horror movie that could be made quickly, cheaply and very simply. It became *The Hills Have Eyes*.

On one level *The Hills Have Eyes* was a less graphic, more user-friendly *Last House*. It was about a nice, suburban American family, whose camper van breaks down in the desert and who are then attacked by the members of another family – a bunch of in-bred cannibals. As in *Last House*, the nice family turns nasty after one of them is killed and another abducted, and they wreak bloody vengeance on their attackers. It's a violent piece, but without anything like the intensity of the violence in *Last House*. The approach is more like that of an EC horror comic of the Fifties – not that Craven had been allowed to read EC comics as a child. Ironically, the EC horror comics were the main target of the anti-comic-book campaign in America in the Fifties and subsequently banned.

Shot on 16mm, with a budget of $230,000, *The Hills Have Eyes* (1977) made a profit, but more importantly for Craven, it led to more offers of work. (His former partner, Sean Cunningham, was to achieve a major success when he also returned to the horror genre, with *Friday the 13th* in 1980.) One assignment was the opportunity to direct, for NBC, a TV movie starring Linda Blair called *Stranger in Our House* (1978) – released theatrically outside the US as *Summer of Fear*. Based on a novel by Lois Duncan (another of whose novels would provide the basis of Kevin Williamson's *I Know What You Did Last Summer*), it concerned a family who take a distant cousin into their home after her parents are involved in a fatal car accident. The cousin, Julia (Lee Purcell), turns out to be a witch who proceeds to subvert her new family and generally wreak havoc. It was made for network TV as a psychological thriller rather than a horror movie, and contains none of the overt violence that had already become Craven's trademark. He hoped this would prove that he was more than just the maker of horror exploitation movies.

When an Italian producer showed an interest in one of his non-horror projects – a script called *Marimba* about drug smuggling in the jungles of Columbia – he was happy to co-operate, but the film never happened. By now, it was four years since he'd made *Hills* and Craven was anxious to direct a feature film again, so he signed up to make *Swamp Thing*, based on the comic-book character, and almost at the same time became involved in a movie called *Deadly Blessing*.

Thanks to a variety of production problems – a lack of money being the main one – *Swamp Thing* ended up becoming something of a disaster, though an entertaining one. More interesting was *Deadly Blessing* (1981), whose subject matter was close to Craven's heart. It was about a fanatical religious sect in a remote rural area and their adverse reaction to the arrival of a young widow, who has inherited a house on the sect's land, and her two college friends (one of them being Sharon Stone in her first film role). Though it's not a personal favourite of Craven's, it's an above-average horror movie, despite the ludicrous ending imposed on Craven by the producers (that infamous duo, Jon Peters and Peter Guber, who later produced *Batman*) involving a giant incubus making a last-minute, and very unlikely, appearance to grab the heroine (Maren Jensen). It was a blatant attempt to replicate the famous ending of *Carrie*, and it was not the last time that Craven was to have producers trying to impose endings on him. But, ending apart, *Deadly Blessing* marked a new level of sophistication in Craven's directing, demonstrating that he was learning his craft while developing his own unique style at the same time.

While *Deadly Blessing* was only moderately successful at the box office, the shambolic *Swamp Thing* (1982) was a box-office flop. This had a negative effect on Craven's career, and the situation wasn't helped by yet another backlash against the horror film genre (they come in cycles). It certainly wasn't the right time to try and sell a truly innovative horror script that he'd written after making *Swamp Thing* – something called *A Nightmare on Elm Street*. Craven took the project all over Hollywood, and got rejections from everyone. Finally Bob Shaye, president of the relatively small outfit, New Line Cinema, showed some interest and said he'd do it if he could raise the money.

Money was once again Craven's chief source of concern: he was running out of the stuff and no one was offering him any work. And he was now 45. So when Peter Locke approached him and suggested a sequel to *The Hills Have Eyes*, Craven was in no position to say no, even though the idea didn't appeal to him. He wrote the screenplay while Locke raised the finance. Unfortunately, the budget fell far short of what was necessary for Craven to do justice to his own screenplay. 'It was incredibly underfunded,' said Craven, 'so I feel that the script was much better than the film I made based on it. I'm sorry about the way it turned out, but I was dead broke and needed to do any film. I would have done *Godzilla Goes to Paris*.' While still working on *The Hills Have Eyes Part II*, Craven received an offer to do another made-for-TV movie, *Invitation to Hell*, which he eagerly accepted. As a result, after a period of famine he found himself making two pictures at once.

Meanwhile, Robert Shaye at New Line Cinema had finally, after two years, raised the necessary finance for *A Nightmare on Elm Street*. Apart from the *Scream* movies, *Nightmare* is probably the film that Craven will best be remembered for. Utilizing his life-long interest in dreams, and combining it with his love of surrealist cinema, which began with his introduction to the films of Buñuel and Cocteau at college, Craven came up with a truly original concept for a horror movie. The idea of a killer who invades the dreams of his victims and turns them into a physical reality, with fatal results, is something that taps into a primal fear with which we can all identify. Add to that the extra twist that waking up doesn't save you from the threat because the killer can pursue you into *your* reality and finish the job he's started, and you have a definite winner. Which is what *A Nightmare on Elm Street* turned out to be.

However, much to Craven's justified annoyance, another film with a similar theme, *Dreamscape*, was released by Paramount in the same year as *Nightmare* (1984). Craven suspects that *Dreamscape* 'drew inspiration' from his ideas in *Nightmare*, his screenplay having been in circulation for a number of years. 'Everybody in the industry knew about *A Nightmare on Elm Street* three years before we made the movie... the script had been submitted to virtually every studio in Hollywood.' Ironically, the scriptwriter of *Dreamscape*, Charles Russell, would make his directorial debut on the third *Nightmare* movie, *Dream Warriors*.

A Nightmare on Elm Street was both a critical and commercial success, and once again Craven hoped that he'd been provided with the opportunity to break out of the horror genre and enter the mainstream of the film industry. But, as before, things didn't work out that way. Nor had the success of *Nightmare* made him financially secure: he did subsequently receive his share of the movie's profits but he'd directed it for the minimum Directors' Guild fee. And he didn't own the rights to his concept – he'd been obliged to sell them to New Line. 'I was virtually broke when I made *Nightmare*. New Line bought it outright and owned the whole thing.' Considering how much money the company was to make from all the *Nightmare* sequels, Craven has good reason to regret losing control of his creation.

To be fair to New Line, Robert Shaye did ask Craven to direct the first sequel, but he was unhappy with the script and turned the offer down. In the meantime, Craven had directed some episodes for the revived *The Twilight Zone* TV series in 1985 and was still trying to set up non-horror projects. One of these was a TV movie about a bunch of circus children, but nothing ever came of it. He did direct a TV movie for CBS TV that year – *Chiller*, which was about a man cryogenically frozen for ten years who, on being thawed, has lost his soul. Then, in 1986, he planned to make a film of Virginia Andrews' best-selling novel *Flowers in the Attic*. He wrote a screenplay for it, but had to abandon the project; it was later made by someone else. That same year he took a directing assignment based on someone else's script, and by the end of the experience he sincerely wished he hadn't. The film was *Deadly Friend*, and, curiously, it shared a theme with *Chiller*, the TV movie he'd directed. In *Deadly Friend* a teenage genius uses electronic spare parts, including a robot brain, to resurrect the girl he's fallen in love with, after she's been murdered by her father. But, as usual with films dealing with bringing people back from the dead, she lacks a soul. She also displays homicidal tendencies not present in her previous incarnation. The girl was played by newcomer Kristy Swanson who, ironically, went on to appear in *Flowers in the Attic*, and later starred in the 1992 *Buffy the Vampire Slayer* movie.

When Warner Brothers test-screened the film, pushing it as a Wes Craven horror movie, the horror fans reacted with disappointment, so the studio demanded rewrites and the shooting of new footage in order to insert more blood and gore. The finished version of *Deadly Friend* was a mess in more ways than one and left Craven feeling very dissatisfied. However, one good thing did come out of the making of the film: he worked for the first time with Marianne Maddalena, who has been his producer/artistic partner ever since. 'We think alike and we're great pals,' said Craven. 'The combination of the two of us doing a film together seems to be a winning formula. It makes a lot of people happy to work with us. I attribute a lot of that to Marianne herself. She is very smart, enormously capable, but also extremely warm and personable.'

When he was still working on *Deadly Friend*, Robert Shaye of New Line approached Craven and asked him to direct the second *Nightmare* sequel, much to his surprise. He couldn't accept the directing offer because of *Friend*, but he did suggest an idea for the story. Shaye and his colleagues at New Line liked it, so Craven agreed to write the screenplay. It wasn't just because he wanted to see his creation put back on the right track; Craven had another motive – money. 'I was able to negotiate a percentage point in the sequels that I didn't have in the original films.' Craven also took an executive producing credit on the film. 'My understanding was that I'd be asked about things... I'd be brought into casting and have a real creative part in the picture.' But it was not to be.

Craven wrote the screenplay for what would become *A Nightmare on Elm Street Part Three: Dream Warriors* in collaboration with Bruce Wagner, but once he'd delivered the script everything went quiet. Too quiet. 'The reality was that New Line never really contacted me again once they had the script. Then they changed it quite drastically in some ways. A lot of the reasons why I'd agreed to do the picture were taken away.' Craven decided, somewhat bitterly, that the only reason New Line had approached him was that they just wanted his name on another *Nightmare* movie.

But Craven had other things on his mind by then. He'd been approached by a company who'd bought the rights to a non-fiction book by an anthropologist, Wade Davis, called *The Serpent and the Rainbow*. It was the supposedly true story of Wade's experiences in Haiti, when he was investigating the island's many legends about the existence of zombies. Wade had been commissioned by a pharmaceutical company to discover if there was a drug-linked explanation. Craven read Wade's book and immediately agreed to make the movie because it involved so many of his favourite obsessions – the exploration of states of drug-induced consciousness, hallucinations and dreams, and the blurring between reality and fantasy. 'I signed on right away without seeing the script,' he said. 'I knew from the book that anything made from it would be wonderful.'

The film that Craven did make from Wade's book – though it departed from it pretty radically – was interesting, very bizarre and undeniably entertaining, though to describe it as 'wonderful' might be stretching things a little. But when it was released in January of 1988, after a tough location shoot in Haiti, it received good reviews and went on to gross nearly $20 million at the American box office. Craven's instincts about this dubious-sounding project had paid off. And on the back of this success, he signed a two-picture deal with a company called Alive Films, which had a distribution arrangement with Universal.

Even the acrimonious break-up of his five-year marriage to Mimi Meyer-Craven, formerly Millicent Meyer, an actress and model whom he met on a plane in 1983 when she was working as a flight attendant, didn't dent his optimism. Craven was determined to use his deal with Alive Films, and Universal, to come up with a movie that would replicate his *Nightmare* success. He intended to create a villain as popular as Freddy Krueger and thus set up the opportunity for another valuable horror franchise. The big difference would be that this time Craven would be entitled to a large slice of the financial pie. The result was *Shocker*, a film about a murderer called Horace Pinker who, after being executed in the electric chair, is transformed into a malign entity who can take over people's bodies via their TV sets.

It wasn't as original an idea as *Nightmare*, being merely a variation on the old theme of possession, but visually *Shocker* was both ambitious and innovative, especially in the scenes involving television in the last third of the film where the hero, Jonathan Parker (Peter Berg) and Horace Pinker (Mitch Pileggi) fight a duel that spreads right across the prime-time American TV schedule, the pair of them becoming amusingly integrated into various TV shows. 'We had a great deal of fun with the flexibility of video in opticals,' said Craven. 'There's one scene where the hero picks up a TV remote control and beeps the shit out of Pinker, making him reverse, freeze, fast-forward and everything else.' But executing the crucial special effects sequences turned into a real-life nightmare for Craven. He'd delegated the responsibility for the complex opticals to a person who'd made great claims about what he could do. 'It was an innovative new process,' said Craven, 'by which we'd be pulling mattes from film transferred to video at a fraction of the cost.' In theory, that is. The person concerned kept making excuses as to why the work wasn't ready – and then came the shock revelation:

> *He kept saying there were minor problems and he'd give us all the scenes at once... Then we went to dinner with him and he just burst out crying and said it was not working. We should have killed him... Then there was a mad scramble to re-do all the opticals. All the negative had been lost in one way or another and the guy had virtually had a nervous breakdown. We were finding negative under work benches in his lab, in the trunk of his car... It was total chaos.*

Despite this setback *Shocker* was completed and released on schedule, but wasn't successful enough to fulfil Craven's hopes that it would be the start of a long-running series, so he turned his attention back to television. First, he created a comedy series called *The People Next Door* for CBS in 1989, but it was short-lived. Craven then made a TV movie called *Night Visions* for NBC, about a tough LAPD cop, who teams up with a young woman who is just out of college and also happens to be psychic. Craven had hopes that the two-hour movie would serve as the pilot for a series, but it didn't happen. He then came up with a TV project called *Nightmare Café*, which actually got past the pilot stage. 'It's a concept about two people who inherit a café that's somewhere between life and death,' said Craven. 'Sort of like "*Cheers* meets *The Twilight Zone*".' But NBC TV cancelled the series after a short run.

With his next feature film, *The People under the Stairs* in 1991, Craven had a much-needed box-office success. The idea came from a newspaper story that Craven had spotted back in 1978 about a couple who'd kept their children locked up for years in their home. From that basic concept Craven concocted a weird, modern fairy tale about a man and woman, both terrifyingly crazy, who keep a whole tribe of brutalized children trapped in the basement of their vast, booby-trap-filled house. Craven intended it to be a political allegory, but to the general audience it was just an above-average horror movie – fortunately. It grossed over $24 million in America and would count as his most financially successful film until *Scream*.

Late in 1992 Craven had a fateful meeting with Robert Shaye of New Line, during which they buried the hatchet – in the nicest possible way. Craven expressed his dissatisfaction with the way he felt he'd been treated by New Line on the financial side of the *A Nightmare on Elm Street* series. Shaye reacted sympathetically to Craven's list of grievances and promised to deal with them, which he did. According to Craven, 'In the subsequent month he made good on all the things I felt had been left unattended. There were significant payments and the beginning of a very uniform accounting of profits and so forth.' In the light of this new, mutually happy, relationship, Craven reacted positively when Shaye asked him to consider making another Freddy Krueger movie. The result was to be *Wes Craven's New Nightmare*.

Now in creative control, Craven set out to make a movie quite unlike all the previous episodes of the *Nightmare* series, and which was to foreshadow the *Scream* movies in certain ways. Not only did *Wes Craven's New Nightmare* introduce a post-modernist approach to horror, but in setting it in the film industry and dealing with the making of a Freddy movie in 'real life', it anticipated similar devices used in *Scream*s 2 and 3. 'The simple way to put it,' said Craven, 'is, what if New Line stopped making the *Nightmare* series and unintentionally released the spirit of Freddy to go where he will, and he decides to cross over into our reality. His only limitation is that he must pass through the actress who played the character who first defeated him.'

Heather Langenkamp, the star of the first film, agreed to return to play herself, as did Robert Englund (Freddy). And as the film would be set in New Line's actual production offices, it meant that certain New Line people would also be required to play themselves, including the company's head, Robert Shaye. 'After his scenes were shot,' said Craven, 'he immediately started talking about reshoots because he thought he was terrible. In fact, he was quite good.' Wes Craven also played himself, as did his producer, Marianne Maddalena. Other cast members from the first *Nightmare* who joined Langenkamp and Englund in this unusual acting exercise were John Saxon, Nick Corri and Tuesday Knight.

Apart from having a dig at the film industry, *New Nightmare* also enabled Craven to get in a few jabs at his old adversaries, the film censors at the MPAA. 'There is a lot of humour in the film and skewering of various people. There's a strong treatment of the "Do horror films harm or help children" debate. A central figure is called Dr Heffner, which was the name of the guy who headed the MPAA. Heather's young son in the film has what appears to be a nervous breakdown, which the Dr Heffner character blames on him having seen Heather's films.'

Wes Craven's New Nightmare is undoubtedly a very clever film, but it might have been too clever for its own good. When it was released on 7 October 1994 it received a favourable reaction from the critics, but cinema audiences weren't as kind. In box-office terms it was the least successful of all the *Nightmare* movies.

As Randy says in *Scream*, 'If it's too complicated, you lose your target audience.'

Finding the right target audience turned out to be a serious problem with Craven's next film, *Vampire in Brooklyn* (1995). Craven was flattered to be asked by Eddie Murphy to direct his new film, based on an idea that Eddie and his brother Charlie had devised. He would not only be working with a major Hollywood star for the first time in his career, he'd also be making his first big studio picture (for Paramount). Craven was also flattered when he learned that Murphy was a big fan of his pictures, in particular *The Serpent and the Rainbow*.

Designed to be the first black vampire movie since *Blacula*, back in the early Seventies, *Vampire* was about Murphy's vampire character, Max, coming to Brooklyn to find the woman destined to become his vampire queen. The object of his quest turns out to be Rita (Angela Bassett), a dedicated cop with a complicated relationship with her police partner, Warren (Allen Payne). The main problems with the making of the film centred on the fact that everyone involved with it had different views on what sort of movie it should be. Craven hoped he would be making a comedy with comedy star Eddie Murphy, while Murphy hoped he would be making a straight horror movie with horror maestro, Wes Craven. As for the Paramount executives, they were determined to get a comedy from Murphy, despite his firm resistance to go in a different direction. Needless to say, the two writers, Chris Parker and Michael Lucker, brought in to unify and polish the final screenplay, had a difficult task in giving all the different parties what they wanted.

Probably most accurately described as an 'interesting failure', it's in the area of comedy that *Vampire in Brooklyn* works best: one amusing sub-plot concerns a local man who becomes Max's undead slave and has to cope with pieces of his anatomy dropping off at inconvenient moments throughout the film. But Paramount didn't get the comedy blockbuster they were hoping for. It only grossed $20 million in the US and the reviewers were only too keen to point out that the film was neither fish nor fowl – neither an Eddie Murphy movie nor a Wes Craven one.

Disappointed with the response to *Vampire*, Craven again declared his wish to move out of the horror ghetto: '*Vampire* was a little step out, but since it wasn't a big financial success it probably didn't help my career any. I don't think I'll be getting offers to do more comedy.'

But what he did get after that was an offer from Miramax to direct *Scream* (a comedy of sorts) – and at the age of 57, he enjoyed the sort of success that had been denied him in his career until then. Ironically, though *Scream* owed a lot to *Halloween*, and Kevin Williamson wrote the screenplay as a homage to that film, Craven was never that enthusiastic about the John Carpenter classic. 'It was good,' said Craven, 'but I'm not a huge fan of *Halloween*. I was always aware of it being out there, and being one of my competitors and having a very strong following. It was a very straightforward film that didn't make any apologies for being exactly what it was, and nothing more. Sometimes that kind of film can be very power-ful. I think *Friday the 13th* was like that.'

After *Scream 2*, and before he started work on *Scream 3*, Craven unwisely had his name associated with two other horror films. One of them was the tacky *Wishmaster* (1997), a sub-*Hellraiser* movie with lots of gore but no imagination. The film was released as *Wes Craven's Wishmaster* though he was only an executive producer. Presumably he became involved in the project as a favour to the director, Robert Kurtzman, a former effects make-up man who worked on *Scream*. The other film was the dismal 1999 remake of *Carnival of Souls*, directed by Adam Grossman.

Craven's excuse was that he liked the original and thought it would be fun to do a remake of it. But he said, 'I think it needs a bit more story, so you clearly know who that person is walking around in that spooky place.' The 1962 *Carnival of Souls*, an independent production made on an almost non-existent budget by one-off film-maker Herk Harvey, was an eerie little film about a young woman who survives a car crash and is then plagued by menacing appari-tions. It's only at the end of the movie – in a plot-device revived by *The Sixth Sense* – that she discovers she's been dead ever since the crash. Much of its charm comes from its threadbare production values and its obvious amateur status, and it's deservedly regarded as a cult classic, whereas the remake, on which Craven acted in an 'advisory capacity', is a badly-made, and entirely redundant, travesty of the original.

But the film closest to Craven's heart was his long-planned non-horror, art-house effort, *Music of the Heart*, which was also made between *Screams 2* and *3*. It is based on an Oscar-winning documen-tary called *Small Wonders* about Roberta Guaspari, who established a highly successful music programme at a Harlem grade school. 'It's happened for me, but it's taken 25 years,' said Craven in 1997. 'I think it's going to be called *Fiddlefest* [it wasn't], so it will be a case of going from violence to fiddles, and it will be very different from what I've done before [it was]. We're just getting the first drafts of the scripts and Madonna is attached to star in it [she didn't].'

Scripted by Pamela Gray, the film starred Meryl Streep, who'd agreed to play Roberta Guaspari when Madonna pulled out of the project after a disagreement with Craven on how the role should be played. Amusingly, Streep was upfront with Craven on what she thought of his horror movies, telling him that she couldn't understand why people would want to go and see such films. Craven tried to persuade her to make a cameo appearance in *Scream 3*, but she refused. *Music of the Heart* opened in America in October 1999 and was greeted with poor reviews (though Streep received praise) and apathy from cinema-goers. Reviewers criticized its poor construction, pacing, dialogue and even Gloria Estefan's theme song. Predictably, one reviewer said that having Freddy Krueger leap out from behind a piano would have provided welcome relief. On the week of its release it did reach number five in the American box-office chart, but subsequently faded from view very swiftly. It's unlikely that Miramax will see a return on their investment but the company probably didn't expect to. As one critic said, *Music of the Heart* is Craven's vanity project financed by the Weinstein brothers as a payback for all the money that the *Scream* movies made for Miramax.

Now that Craven has got *Music of the Heart* out of his system, will he be satisfied to return to the horror genre? It doesn't seem likely. He hopes that his next project will be a film version of his novel, *Fountain Society*, to which Dreamworks have bought the film rights and which he insists is not really a genre subject, despite its strong science-fiction elements: 'It's more of a Michael Crichton medical thriller,' says Craven. If *Scream 3* proves to be as big a success as its two predecessors he's going to have to face the fact, distasteful though it may be to him, that in the public's perception the name 'Wes Craven' is going to remain synonymous with horror, no matter what he tries to do to change it. *Scream 3* may well mark the end of the *Scream* series, as everyone concerned, including Craven, insists that it will – but if he wants another box-office success beyond *Scream*, he's not going to achieve it with a movie like *Music of the Heart*...

His core audience is never going to let him go.

BIBLIOGRAPHY

BOOKS

The Nightmare on Elm Street by Jeffrey Cooper
(St Martins Press, 1987)

Screams and Nightmares by Brian J. Robb
(Titan Books, 1998)

Wes Craven's Last House on the Left by David A. Szulkin
(FAB Press, 1997)

MAGAZINES

Cinefantastique
Directors Guild of America Magazine
Empire
Fade In
Fangoria
Journal of Popular Film and Television
Movieline
Premiere
Screen International
Starburst
Total Film
Vanity Fair
Variety